Who says it's a woman's job to clean?

Don Aslett

EXLEY

ALSO BY DON ASLETT:
Is there life after housework?
How to win at housework
Freedom from clutter

Published in 1986 by
Exley Publications Ltd,
16 Chalk Hill, Watford,
Herts WD1 4BN.

First published in the USA by Writer's
Digest Books.

Copyright © 1986 Don Aslett

**Printed and bound in Great Britain by
Hazell Watson & Viney Ltd.**

*British Library Cataloguing in Publication
Data.*
Who says it's a woman's job to clean?
1. Home economics
I. Aslett, Don
648'.024041 TX324

ISBN 1-85015-048-6
ISBN 1-85015-049-4 Pbk

ILLUSTRATIONS BY DAVID LOCK

3.

Contents

Dad – is this when Mum
came to clean for us?

Introduction

The smell of burning brooms first drifted into the air during the late sixties. Most of us men ignored the chant of demands and shrank quietly out of sight, waiting for the calm of unquestioned house bondage to come back, for the rebellion to be over.

At the time, I saw all this as a sad waste of good cleaning equipment, because I was a struggling student who depended on a broom to earn money for me while I was at university.

Now, after thirty years as a professional cleaner, writing four books and conducting hundreds of public appearances on the subject of cleaning, I've even been called the "World's Number One Cleaning Expert". But "famous cleaner" or not, I'm sure that in attitude and performance you and I perform al-most equally around the house. We men are so much alike it's almost uncanny. I try to tell my wife she got a better deal than other wives because I'm so dynamic, handsome and in demand, and she tells me that I sound and act just like the rest of the males bouncing around the world.

The only difference is that from my exposure to the hundreds of thousands of women in my house-cleaning seminars and the millions in my reading and viewing audiences, I've learned a few things that have finally caused me to surrender some of my male slobbism and snobbism and be a little more helpful around the house.

For years now, women have been trapped behind enemy lines. Lines of dishes, lines of dirty floors, lines of leaking taps, lines of kids, lines

of family excuses. Women are pinned down; they know the problem and they need performance, not sympathy.

I wrote this book because I wanted men to understand what women have been trying to say to them for years. I don't believe it's "her" job to get others around the house to clean – through trickery, bribery, coaxing or seduction. And I'm convinced that the only reason men are still dumping the housework on women is that they've never really thought about the unfairness of it all. I realize you were cheated out of the chance to clean – your mother never taught you – but I'm brash enough to believe I can teach you better than your mother ever could.

Your desire to be a better person, a fair person, a macho man or a re-nowned gentleman will be immeasurably advanced by reading and using the material in the following pages. Every man has a secret mission to correct some social wrong. He yearns for the chance to put the world right, whether it be helping an orphan or giving a chance on the team to Casper Ten Thumbs. No wrong needs correction more than the unequal division of home chores and duties. Talk about a chance for glory and self-esteem! I promise you that nothing will be nobler than saving a woman from a dirty dish at the end of a discouraging day. Try it – you'll be amazed how much you like it.

P.S. You few who do do your share (or more) of housework: if your wife doesn't appreciate you, make her read this book.

Don A. Aslett

Chapter One

How could a man know anything about cleaning?

Let me introduce myself before I let you in on what I've learned ... about being a real man around the house.

When I was an energetic twenty-year-old, fresh off the farm and eager to find a way to pay my way through university, a friend told me I should consider being a professional cleaner. "There isn't a woman in the world who doesn't need help with the housework." "How do you do it?" I asked. "Just put an ad in the paper, and the women will phone you."

A housecleaner is born

Before I knew it, I found myself with a chimney sweeping job, followed by some floors, then some windows. Next came wall washing and cupboard cleaning, carpet and upholstery care. On every job, the women would coach and direct me, and I would scrub, shovel and polish.

Soon I was putting on a white uniform after my afternoon classes, knocking on doors and asking if I could assume some of the household drudgery. Word got around that there was an eager housecleaner loose in the neighbourhood, and soon I had more work than I could handle. I hired fellow students to help and taught them what the homemakers had taught me.

I didn't think much then about the pressures and demands on women for cleaning, because the harder it was for them to cope with it and the more they hated it, the better my business was. And the women sang our praises as we diligently de-grimed their ceilings and uncluttered their cupboards.

In the next ten years, my house-cleaning business received a good deal of notice – *"University Boy Makes Good."* Between newspaper headlines I acquired a lot of experi-

11

ence in housecleaning methods. I ruined grand piano tops, knocked over china cabinets, broke windows, streaked walls, damaged pictures, shrank wall-to-wall carpets into rugs, and made scores of other goofs. But with each job I got better and faster and more efficient (at cleaning, not breaking!). I cleaned log cabins and plush mansions. I cleaned up after fires, floods, vandals, suicides and after husbands whose wives had been away for a few days. Sometimes I would have five crews working at once and my business grew steadily into a large professional organization cleaning houses, shops, banks and factories.

By the time I graduated, I realized that I knew more about cleaning toilets than I did about dissecting frogs, so I decided to stay in the business. I got a few other graduates of pharmacy and psychology to manage my company and began to build it into what it is today, one of America's top cleaning firms. I got quite good at cleaning in the process, and some of you may have seen me on TV demonstrating professional cleaning methods. Or your wife may have read one of my other books and started raving about how she learned to save her cleaning time.

The reason I made sense to your wives is because my wife finally got to me. Seven years ago she did me a big favour by having my scout troop over and cooking for them; I told her the next time she had a church or community responsibility I would return the favour. Within a month she announced that the theme for her church women's next mini-lesson was "The Art of Organized Cleaning". Would I give a presentation showing some professional secrets they could use in the home to save time and do a better job? As any of you would, I jumped at the chance to perform for a group of lovely ladies. I built a little house for a visual aid, and taught a humorous one-hour session. After I finished I felt like Elvis Presley; they rushed at me, nearly ripping off my buttons and begged for more material. Now, when you've been a cleaner – and a toilet cleaner – for eighteen years and you are suddenly mobbed by sixty women, you say to yourself, 'Wow, this is living!'. So I gave another talk and then another, each time adding a few more professional approaches and techniques and introducing the women to new professional tools. My audiences grew from 50 to 100, to 300 and then 900; my presentation stretched to three hours. I had a waiting list of people who wanted me to give demonstrations and talks. At every one, the women in my audience would sit hypnotized because someone was showing them how to cut that most dreaded and unrewarding word, housework, out of their vocabulary.

This much impressed me as did the fact that there seemed to be little real information about cleaning available anywhere, only the old wives' tales handed down from generation to generation, and a few household hint and tip books. So I sat down and wrote a book, *Is There Life After Housework?*

Soon I was doing radio and TV shows and by November of 1982, *Is There Life After Housework?* made it to the bestseller list in the USA and for ten days was even ahead of *The Joy of Sex* and *Thirty Days to a Beautiful Bottom*.

One hint that *Is There Life After Housework?* overlooked and a subject that had been looked down on for centuries, was a hot subject.

A feature of the book that always brought shrieks of laughter from my audience was Chapter 5, "What to Expect from Your Husband and Children" – after a handsome introductory illustration came nothing but blank pages. Although I did this – and even chose the title of the book itself – to let women know that I understood and sympathized with their problem, I gave them nothing more than a chuckle. I only paid lip service to the problem when you consider

what I myself was still doing around our house. I sensed that my wife really did a lot, and my heart went out to her, but my hands didn't go into the washing-up water. Like most of our wives, mine got lots of appreciation and occasionally even roses, but still not much help.

True, like you maybe, I did the painting and repairing and the heavy work, but the food, clothes, floors, children, etc. – ninety per cent of it was still, sad to say, the woman's job. I was providing a living – yet I still had time to go fishing, play tennis or just swan around. I'd work late at the office, watch the news on TV, then stagger off to bed – leaving my shoes, books, papers, empty crisp packets and empty glass right where I'd been sitting.

Most of us think we do a great deal, but in fact, on average we are negative producers. We don't even clean up our own personal mess and projects, much less help out with the mess caused by others.

A housecleaner is reborn

Since she's married to a well-known and successful cleaning professional, you can imagine what the first and most frequently asked question is of my wife Barbara. You've guessed it: "Does he do the cleaning at home?" And you can bet that the more times she's asked this the more conscious I become of what I do (and don't do) at home. After all, I know how, why, when and what to do in every area of cleaning and I even write books about it. The truth is, I still have to kick and nudge and prod myself to keep myself aware of my output in the housework department. There *are* some tough habits to overcome here. For decades, hundreds, even thousands of years, housework was magically performed for us. We just had to get up from the table and hey presto, all the dirty dishes were soon clean and stacked in the cupboard. We only had to throw our dirty clothes in a basket (or a pile) and snap, they reappeared clean and pressed and neatly hanging in the wardrobe. If we noticed a spot or spill, we only had to twitch our nose or wrinkle our brow, ignore it ourselves a little longer and zap, it was gone! Some of us got so used to this female magic that we even expected the woman of the house to pay the bills without giving her enough money to do it.

My repentance really started when I began handing out "comment cards" at my seminars. The responses from the 180,000 women who attended were eye-opening, especially the answers to the question "Percentage of work done by spouse". Rich or poor, foreign or American, working or stay-at-homers, every woman filled it in the same: "0". Some would even cross out the "0" and mark "–10%". The comments were pleading, confused, pathetic – even aggressive – but they all said the same thing: "No one knows what is going on and no one helps."

For the first time in my life, I began to look at myself and what I saw wasn't very nice. I was one of the very people these women were complaining about. I would try on three shirts for my "big publicity tour" and leave two on the bed. I was too lazy to launder my dirty clothes or to wash up my own dishes after a meal when my wife was out. I never turned my socks right side out. I didn't even know how to use the washing machine.

And whose example did my six children follow? Their father's, of course. School clothes, scout gear, craft projects, curlers, toys, etc., were strewn all over our nice new home. You know the morning rush and scramble to get to work and school – after everyone's gone the woman walks into a room that looks as if a hand grenade has hit it. Two hours at the very beginning of the day wiped out – and for whose mess? Disgraceful, don't you think? Yet I, a famous cleaning expert, was doing it. I thought I was a nice bloke and I loved my wife, but I deprived her of several hours of her day, every day, through carelessness and inconsideration.

I'd also spent a lot of time in my professional speaking engagements, trying to raise the self-esteem of professional full-time cleaners. I know how put down and put upon they feel, even though they're doing a job that civilization couldn't do without. I'd even publicly bemoaned the fact that "the cleaner" is treated like a piece of furniture. Then one day it dawned on me that the image of "cleaning" – in the world of professional cleaning and the home – is the same. People leave the building in the evening, leaving rubbish, ash, debris, and dirtied, smeared, crumpled, rumpled things. Then the cleaners appear like phantoms in the night and in the morning all is restored, ready to use and mess up again. It's the same at home – everyone takes all the positive for granted and notices only the negative.

The cleaning efforts of this world, at work and home, just aren't recognized and appreciated. They're not shared and they're not respected. My professional (and now *home*) goal is to change that.

Chapter Two

What's been going on?

I've seen a few books and articles that claim men are doing more housework. I guess five per cent is better than nothing, but in truth men are not doing much more than they ever did.

Evidence

There are *men-vs-women* studies, polls, predictions, analyses. They speculate and make assumptions and often contradict each other, but none of them give us any information we can't see for ourselves.

We don't need charts and certificates of proof – we see it and live it every day of the week. The evidence is in front of our eyes, everywhere. Ninety per cent of housework is caused by men and children: ninety per cent of cleaning up is done by women. We expect it, we allow it, we encourage it and we seldom appreciate it. That's it – pure and simple.

If you want evidence, just look around: at family, relatives, neighbours. The woman is assigned to clean up after everyone, and the mess is always the woman's problem. She can be a real worker, a fast, efficient cleaner and personally immaculate, but married to a mobile mud pie of a man and the judgment on the resulting condition of the house, by everyone (even other unforgiving *women*) is "That woman's house looks terrible!"

Life today is different, more complicated than it's ever been. Many women are breadwinners and their time at home is limited. But even in situations where men are unemployed, looking for a job and hanging around the house, it's as much as they can do to have a shave and take their empty coffee mugs

17

back to the kitchen. Guess who comes home from work and does the cooking, cleaning, and domestic decision making ... *the woman!*

Big healthy men go to university while the wife works, looks after the children, cleans the house, does the shopping and cooking; then the man comes home sighing about how hard his day was and how exhausted he is.

The man has *his* dog and *his* car and *his* clothes until they are dirty, broken or sick and suddenly they become *hers.* The wife takes the dog to the vet, does the washing, runs to the dry cleaner and arranges to get the car mended. Amazing transformation, huh?

At first I couldn't work out the meaning of the squint-eyed look I usually got from the husband when I turned up to do a professional housecleaning job. (After thirty years and cleaning thousands of homes I now understand the look perfectly – it was *guilt!*) Most of the work the women got me to do could have easily been done by the man of the house, who often passed me on his way out to burn off some energy at the squash court.

I've carried box upon box from cellars, walking right past sets of macho muscle-building equipment. I've torn out the broken down old fences and furnishings in homes where the husband owned a pick-up and had three days a week off. I've even been asked by women to build shelves in carpenters' homes. In fact, in all these years I've very seldom done housework for women that they could have handled themselves – it was usually the heavy, the high and the big-equipment jobs. After fifteen years of waiting for their husbands or sons to get round to it, the female decided hiring me was easier than nagging them.

The shoemaker's son syndrome

The fully certified car mechanic has had another successful day. In between routine brake jobs, and carburretor rebuildings, he pulled off a beautiful salvage job on a car there weren't any replacement parts for, and managed to decipher the program on an unfamiliar vehicle's mini-computer. He comes home to discover that his wife's mini is stuck down the road. It's the third time it's broken down this month, the third time he's given it a patch and a promise. Will he fix it properly this time?

A navy officer served up exotic pastries and delicacies all through his stint in the service. He could feed an entire troopship smoothly and without strain because he was a marvel of quality and efficiency in the kitchen. Twenty years later, at home with his wife and family, he bakes and cooks.

The surgeon performs unsurpassed suturing every week. His delicate cuts and stitches are the salvation of the most difficult cases. At home a button pops off his dinner jacket. Does he sew it on?

A noted landscape gardener daily grooms the grounds of the rich and famous, whistling happily all the while. He can design a herb garden or an orchard with ease and even the most finicky greenery thrives at the touch of his trowel. Will he help his wife plant the new rose bush in the back garden?

The award-winning chemist regularly writes up complex reports for prestigious technical journals. If he ever publishes his book he intends to thank his wife, who organizes all his research and does his manuscript typing. At home, does this brilliant man know how to make coffee, operate a tumble dryer, oven or vacuum cleaner?

A father takes his three boys to McDonald's for lunch and they eat and eat. When they're finished they all carefully clean up their mess – all the boxes, wrappers, paper cups and paper bags – and throw it all in the rubbish bin. At supper that night at home they eat and eat. Do they carry their plates to the sink or put even one item in the bin?

20

If every other occupation were added to this list, it would fill this book. Why won't we do these things at home? There's no logical or just excuse:

1. We know how
2. It needs to be done
3. It costs nothing for us to do it
4. We love our home
5. We have the time

It's not lack of pride or even laziness. Nothing speaks louder than action. There's only one reason: We *do* feel that – at home – *it's a woman's job to clean.*

Do to your lady as you do unto others

"My husband will work impossibly long hours for a friend for a charity project or for a political candidate, while the windows fall out of our house. He will cheerfully help out anyone else anywhere in the world."

Remember all those times your mother said to you: "You children treat strangers better than you do your own brothers and sisters" – and we did. We do exactly the same thing with housework. While at someone else's house we will politely pick up our apple cores or break our necks to return the used lemonade glass to the sink, and always when getting up from a meal offer, "May I help?" Four hours later at home, we haven't the vaguest recollection of such action. That makes us downright hypocritical, and more than anything, we hate being *called* a hypocrite. All the things we do at the homes of others and when we're away from home – let's just try to do the same in our own home.

Ignorance, not chauvinism

It's not necessarily chauvinism. Often it's ignorance. Cleaning awareness hardly exists for the average male. Very few men or children are aware of the housework that goes on all the time, right where they live.

I served as leader of a contingent of forty Boy Scouts for three national Jamborees, where more than 30,000 thirteen- to sixteen-year-olds travel to a mass camp for ten days of fun, experience and education. These boys are the cream of the scouting crop, as their rank and the qualifications to attend testify.

But it was like escorting forty

flesh-covered refuse lorries. Every stop, every eating area, every motel room we left was a mass of litter and waste. Ten scouts and their grown leader take a break and what do you find? Eleven soft drink cans! They can expand a single six-pack or snack packet into twenty square feet of rubbish. On the ground under and around every outdoor table were squashed sauce packets, half-eaten food, wrappers, silverware, openers, tools and twisted, wrinkled magazines. I asked one bright-eyed fourteen-year-old: "Doesn't this mess bother you?" His answer: "I didn't notice it."

Boys' and leaders' tents alike looked like someone had eggbeatered a Salvation Army storeroom and dumped it a foot deep on the floor. Most of them would run completely out of socks, underwear and money before giving a thought to replacements. Every burnt-out torch bulb, crumpled tissue and dead ball-point was dropped, left, or laid just where it was finished with. And remember we're talking about *scouts* here – clean, healthy, honourable, well-disciplined, good family lads.

And it's not just children. Young men go off to university to learn how to manage a business when they can't even manage the aftermath of their own daily grooming. A colonel at one army base told me, "Don, I have thousands of people living here and almost none of them know how to clean when they get here. Someone has always done it for them at home, at school and at work. They think a floor stripper is the girl who dances at the night club."

It's time for equality of vocabulary

I fumed and roared about ten years ago, when the equality thing hit my business and I had to go through everything and "de-sex" it – change the "man" in salesman, doorman, etc., and stop assuming, in my literature, that all managers were "he's". But the more I did it, the more logical it seemed, and soon it even felt natural to think of a job as neutral in gender when in fact it was.

Now it occurs to me that we ought to finish the job and get the word "woman" out of the just-as-neutral roles of home and housework. "Hers" and "house" have become synonymous; home and housework terminology is so femanised it almost needs a court ruling to abolish it.

Consider:
Housewife

Cleaning lady

Charwoman

Mother's little helper

A woman's place is in the home

A woman's work is never done

"Her kitchen", "your cupboards", "your washing machine"

"Where do you keep the bleach, dear?"

"Mother's Pride"

"That's woman's work"

"Mum's home cooking"

"She can't cook, but I love her anyway"

"Darling, I'm home ... Where's dinner?"

"Don't cook anything tonight, sweetheart – I'll take you out to eat."

"Where've you put my socks?"

"When you pack my clothes, make sure you put my blue shorts in."

"I bought you a new vacuum cleaner for your birthday."

"This place is always so untidy!"

"Go and ask your mother."

"You're working on Saturday! Who's going to look after the kids?"

"Can't you get these children to keep their rooms clean?"

"Can't you keep them quiet?"

"I did your washing-up for you."

Isn't it time we took the "y" off *your?*

It's going to take a while to cut the cords of tradition whereby the girls forever did the inside work and the boys did the outside work. *Why?* Not one reason in the world other than it was handed down; mother did what

her mother did, what her grand-mother did and what her great-grand-

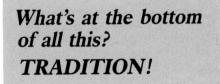

What's at the bottom of all this? TRADITION!

mother did. Twenty years ago, forty years ago, it was traditional that women did the cleaning and men made the living for the household. Now many women are contributing financially to support the family, and yet few men are doing housework. Men expect women to clean because their mothers did. Women feel guilty

24

about not cleaning because their mothers did.

The TV ads aren't helping. Ever noticed that it's always men who are making the appraisal of the clean shirts, the good food, etc. – but who is doing the work? Notice, too, it's always the young wife who purchases the wrong cleaning product and the wise old woman of much experience who tells her a bargain is not necessarily a bargain. It's the daughter, not the son, we are still teaching to carry on the tradition. The male offspring is big enough to play football and bright enough to use a computer, but he's allowed to rush into the house with grass-stained clothes and hand them to his mother. "Here, Mum, wash these!" Give me one – just *one* – good reason why it's a woman's job to clean any more than anyone else's.

It's easy to understand why we men automatically assume we'll be "cleaned up after". Mother and sister did it for us when we were babies (and beyond), caretakers and teachers did it for us at school. The team coach tidied our locker room, the councils clean up the roads and parks after us and take away our rubbish. For a lifetime most of us have been taught that there will always be *someone* (generally a woman) to clean up after us.

We don't have to be intimidated

Honestly, Ma'am – my wife *adores* washing!

by *tradition*. All it means is "the way they did things for a while". The way they did things then may not meet the needs of now. Today men and women do much the same kinds of work outside the home. It only makes sense that we share the same kinds of work *inside* the home, too.

A day in the life of a housecleaner

My reputation as a well-known "cleaning expert" testified that I knew a lot about house*cleaning*, but, like most men, nothing about house*work*.

I still watched, with a certain critical eye, the efforts of my wife and of other women as they struggled feverishly to get the housework accomplished. I ached to jump in and show those "disorganized gals" how an expert could tidy things away. The opportunity soon arrived. Early in our marriage I worked hard washing walls late at night to buy my wife a surprise plane ticket to Alaska. She was delighted to have her first flight ever and a chance to see her mother again. I said goodbye to her and told her to stay as long as she wished; I would take good care of our six small children. She wasted no time leaving, I assure you. My true thoughts were, "Now that I have her out of my way, I'm going to lick this house into shape

and make it as efficient as my business."

I woke up at four the first morning and confidently mapped out the great campaign of household efficiency that was about to be launched in our home. By 6.30 a.m. the kids were up and they saluted before they went to the bathroom! By 7.30 the beds were made, the washing up was done, and I was rolling to victory.

We were putting the finishing touches to a new home, and my project for the day was the construction of a vanity cabinet in the bathroom – an easy half-day's work. I had just started to glue the first board when *Waaa!* One of the kids had biffed another. I ran out, made peace, passed round the storybooks and read a beautiful story. Then I picked up the board again. *Waaa!* Someone had hurt a finger. Three Band-Aids and ten minutes of comforting later, I picked up the hammer (after scraping off the now-dry glue) and had one nail started when *Waaa!* – a nappy to change (a cry which was repeated at intervals all day).

Again I returned to work and had started the second nail when *Ding-Dong*, the milkman. I slammed the cream in the refrigerator, then *Ding-Dong*, the postman. I ran down and signed for a parcel, then *Ring-a-ling*, the school telephoning to ask about registering one of the children for school. It's embarrassing enough when you don't know what a rubella injection is, but when you don't know your own child's birthday, you're an outright scab! Then *Knock-knock*, "Can I borrow ..." Then *Buzz* – time for lunch ... time for bottles. *Waaa* ...! nappies again, etc., etc. You wouldn't believe how my morning went. My building project looked like a chimpanzee special – dried glue and badly cut boards all over, and no real progress had been made.

Noon came and with it, another surprise. Those little monsters don't appreciate what you do for them, all that work cooking and they threw food, slobbered, and not one of them thanked me. I found out that to dress a toddler once was just a warm-up. I re-clothed one of those children four times by 1.15.

Nap time, and would you believe that kids don't all go to sleep at the same time? I've bedded down six hundred head of cattle more easily and quickly than those six kids. When I finally got them all down, no way was I going to hammer, play the stereo, or even turn a page loudly and risk waking them up.

Fortunately, the day ended just before I did. I had two boards up on the cabinet by the time the last baby was ready to sleep. The most famous housecleaner and best organizer in the West had accomplished nothing.

After that first day was over – it was now midnight – I walked into our bedroom and shook and quivered like a man who's just received an income tax demand.

I'd never worked so hard in my life and I was right back where I'd started when I got up. I'd never had that feeling before. A woman lives with it every day. The week before three people had taken me out for dinner, I'd bought four vans with one sweep of the hand, expanded my business with a single phone call – but today I was just tired and discouraged.

I'll skip over the gory details of the next few days – but in general my "half-day" cabinet job, only half-complete, bit the dust. A week later my wife phoned to check on things. I pinched the kids to get them howling in the background so I wouldn't have to beg her to come and save me. She returned at once and I suddenly got efficient again.

Believe it or not, even wives who can devote all their time to home-making have normal days that are worse than our worst. In the "world" of work, jobs are specialized and streamlined so that everyone can work efficiently: secretaries and receptionists answer the phone and otherwise stop their managers being distracted; on a production line, tools and supplies are brought to the assemblers. The homemaker, however, does it all: answers the phone and the door, cleans, cooks and does the washing, all the while minding an infant or a toddler and trying to put new covers on the couch or paint the spare room. The "interruptions" in a homemaker's day can't be ignored or "delegated": the child who was teased on the playground has to be comforted, the neighbour organizing a neighbourhood-watch programme must be listened to, the friend who calls to discuss her problem child can't be ignored. But the homemaker still has to prepare those three meals that get eaten as soon as they're ready and clean that bathroom that immediately gets dirty again. And there's no supervisor to reward the homemaker with a rise or a promotion because she also found the time to grow organic vegetables in the garden, or to teach her four-year-old to read.

We men really pull a fast trick when we, steeped in our business books, inform our wives that they must learn to delegate. Now tell me, gentlemen, who can your wife delegate housework to? You are basically the *only* candidate, because if you don't do housework then the kids (following Daddy's example) certainly won't do any of it. There's no one in the business of housework to delegate to. But we men operate brilliantly at home by a process called Absentee Delegation, which means the body is absent when the work needs to be done.

An ounce of appreciation

Women are actually more embittered about lack of appreciation than about the dirty deal they get on the housework. They say the biggest problem is that when they are tired or overwhelmed by housework, it would be nice to get some understanding and encouragement rather than criticism.

Many women tell me that – unfair as it might be – they would ungrudgingly do all the housework if they received even an ounce of appreciation after it was done, or if someone just *noticed* it'd been done. One woman told me, "I don't care if he does it or not, just as long as he understands."

We men in casual conversation seem to say just the opposite, such as the friend of mine who in front of a group, graciously – even nobly – said "Dear, feel free to stay at home and take care of the house, garden, animals and seven children. No way. No wife of mine is going to work!" Another walked in from work at 5.30 and announced "Why don't you take yourself off to the PTA for an hour? I'll take care of your kids." Could you blame her for nearly exploding and replying, "Jolly nice of you to do that, since I looked after them for you all day."

All hours are equal

A confident husband pulled up in front of a department store, parked his Mercedes carefully, and strolled in. He paused to examine a new bread mixer, advertised to cut bread-making time dramatically. The assistant approached him and politely suggested, "Why don't you buy a bread mixer for your wife?" The man said triumphantly, "Why should I buy one? I *married* a bread mixer."

This kind of attitude is an incredible infringement of one person upon another. We men are undoubtedly the greatest offenders, because traditionally it's been taken for granted that a man's time is worth more than a woman's.

Although I thought I always treated my wife with consideration, I've found myself guilty of the same biases – assuming that her time wasn't worth as much as mine, sending her on errands, assigning her trivial projects because those time-consuming activities were an insult to someone of my ability. A bread mixer, strangely enough, is what woke me up to the equality of hours.

I love homemade bread. Our entire family loves it. Whenever my wife baked bread, it disappeared with

But darling—I <u>am</u> your wages!

gulps and gobbles, without a thank-you, only the question, "When are you baking again?" Eighteen years of married life went by this way, the family prompting, begging and scolding Mum when fresh bread wasn't available.

My wife never asked for a mixer; it was our teenagers who finally persuaded me to buy one. I put up quite a struggle since we were talking about a lot of money for "something for the house!" (I was spending more than that each year on football tickets to tip salespeople I didn't even know.) When we finally got it, and I saw how fast and easily that little machine could turn out scrumptious bread, all I could think of was how much of my wife's time had been wasted – at least two thousand hours – as she kneaded by hand for the past eighteen years.

It wasn't merely the cost of the mixer that postponed the purchase. Like most husbands, I would spend that much on a whim, under the guise of investment or charity. It was total insensitivity to the value of my wife's time. I'd simply assumed it was natural that a woman's time should be taken up with mindless, repetitive tasks. My wife could have used those two thousand hours for herself – to read or relax or play the piano or do something else she would have enjoyed more than pounding piles of dough. It's sad, but when most of us men get a mate to love and cherish for life, we think that some extras come with her. She lives and loves, but she also cooks, sews, cleans, delivers things and shops for us. We fully expect to pay for extra gadgets on a car, but never in our wildest dreams do we expect to pay for the "extras" – work and attention beyond the call of duty – provided by a fellow human being: a woman. If a market value had ever been assigned to housework, and we were charged by the hour – few of us would be able to afford a relationship. Economists have estimated the actual value of the services that go into housework at £16,000 to £28,000 a year. In 1985 Legal and General put the figure for insurance at £254 per week. But because it's never paid, it's never acknowledged.

All hours were created equal. Women's hours have sixty minutes in them, as do *ours*. Too many men think they married a bread mixer, a maid, a gardener, a taxi driver, a nurse, a washerwoman, an errand runner, forgetting that their mate is entitled to the same share of time as they are. For a human being, time is to love, to experience, to feel, to learn, to relax, to accomplish or just to *be*. Position, occupation, status, age and sex don't make any difference.

A few facts you may have missed in the Business News

A 1985 report evaluating a ten-year-long UN campaign to promote equality of the sexes found that women do two-thirds of the world's work, receive a tenth of its income and own less than a hundredth of its property.

From another UN study: The vast array of labour-saving devices in the modern world has not reduced the amount of housework; if anything, it has increased it.

If the value of a wife's services in a home were included in the gross national income, that figure would double in a year.

In February 1985 a survey carried out by the Legal and General Insurance Group showed that a housewife's work was worth £254 per week.

Nine out of ten women work for pay at some time in their lives. Seventy per cent of all women with the youngest child aged 10 or over go to work. (OPCS General Household Survey).

In Social Trends 1985, published by HMSO, it was shown that in 1% of households the ironing was done mainly by men, 10% of ironing was shared equally and in 89% it was done mainly by women. In three per cent of households cleaning was done mainly by men, 24% was equally shared and 72% was done mainly by women.

A Gallup Poll carried out in February 1984 showed that women did 75% of all jobs around the house. That is lower than the HMSO survey, which found that men only did 10% of the housework, and that included families where the mother was working.

Are you holding up your end of the housework? Find out with this test.

Are you a Macho Man?

For each item, rate yourself. Circle your answer and transfer the number to the "Score" column, then add up all the numbers for your total score.

If you live in a flat or maisonette rather than a house (i.e., have no gardening or maintenance to do), add 20 points to your score. If you have no children at home, add 15 points; no pets, add 2 points; no vehicle, add 8.

	Never	Once in a While	50% of the Time	Most of the Time	Always	Score
CLEANING						
I put my own things away	0	1	2	3	5	
I dispose of my old newspapers, magazines & junk mail	0	1	2	3	5	
I clean up my own project mess (sawdust, filings, dirty oil, etc.)	0	1	2	3	5	
I empty my own ashtrays	0	1	2	3	5	
I tidy the house	0	1	2	3	5	

	Never	Once in a While	50% of the Time	Most of the Time	Always	Score
I dust	0	1	2	3	5	
I vacuum	0	1	2	3	5	
I sweep or mop the floors	0	1	2	3	5	
I clean or wash the venetian blinds or curtains	0	1	2	3	5	
I wash the windows	0	1	2	3	5	
I wash the walls	0	1	2	3	5	
I clean the attic and the cellar	0	1	2	3	5	

BED

I make my own bed	0	1	2	3	5	
I make the children's/guest beds	0	1	2	3	5	
I change the sheets	0	1	2	3	5	

BATH

I hang my wet towel up after I shower or bath	0	1	2	3	5	
And wipe or squeegee down the shower walls or wipe out the bath	0	1	2	3	5	
I clean my beard or moustache trimmings out of the sink	0	1	2	3	5	
I clean the toilet	0	1	2	3	5	
I clean the bathroom	0	1	2	3	5	

	Never	Once in a While	50% of the Time	Most of the Time	Always	Score
FOOD						
I clean up after my between-meal snacks	0	1	2	3	5	
I help plan meals	0	1	2	3	5	
I shop for groceries and put them away	0	1	2	3	5	
I cook meals	0	1	2	3	5	
I set the table	0	1	2	3	5	
I clear the table	0	1	2	3	5	
I do the dishes and put them away	0	1	2	3	5	
I help get ready for parties and get-togethers	0	1	2	3	5	
I clean out the fridge and defrost the freezer	0	1	2	3	5	
LAUNDRY						
I hang up my clothes if they're clean enough to wear again	0	1	2	3	5	
I put my dirty clothes in the laundry basket	0	1	2	3	5	
I clean out my pockets and turn my socks and clothes the right side out before I put them in the basket	0	1	2	3	5	
I do the washing	0	1	2	3	5	
And drying	0	1	2	3	5	

	Never	Once in a While	50% of the Time	Most of the Time	Always	Score
I fold laundry and put it away	0	1	2	3	5	
I iron my own shirts	0	1	2	3	5	
I take clothes to the dry cleaner and pick them up	0	1	2	3	5	
I sew on buttons	0	1	2	3	5	

CHILDREN

	Never	Once in a While	50% of the Time	Most of the Time	Always	Score
I play with them and/or take them on outings	0	1	2	3	5	
I discipline them and referee disputes	0	1	2	3	5	
I help out with their school projects	0	1	2	3	5	
I nurse them or take them to the doctor when they're sick	0	1	2	3	5	
I take them shopping for clothes	0	1	2	3	5	
I change their nappies and help with potty training	0	1	2	3	5	
I feed them	0	1	2	3	5	
I give them a bath	0	1	2	3	5	
I go to school meetings, sports days etc.	0	1	2	3	5	
I dress them and help them find their shoes	0	1	2	3	5	
I put them to bed	0	1	2	3	5	

	Never	Once in a While	50% of the Time	Most of the Time	Always	Score
I chauffeur them to their activities	0	1	2	3	5	
I arrange for a babysitter when we need one	0	1	2	3	5	

RUBBISH

	Never	Once in a While	50% of the Time	Most of the Time	Always	Score
I take it out	0	1	2	3	5	
I take it out without being asked	0	1	2	3	5	
I take it to the pavement on collection day	0	1	2	3	5	

MAINTENANCE AND REPAIRS

	Never	Once in a While	50% of the Time	Most of the Time	Always	Score
I do the painting and papering	0	1	2	3	5	
I fix/mend broken things around the house	0	1	2	3	5	
I purchase the parts for household repairs	0	1	2	3	5	
I arrange for repairs if I can't fix something	0	1	2	3	5	
I replace lightbulbs and fuses	0	1	2	3	5	
I tighten hinges, handles and doorknobs	0	1	2	3	5	
I catch and dispose of mice and insects	0	1	2	3	5	

	Never	Once in a While	50% of the Time	Most of the Time	Always	Score
OUTSIDE						
I mow the lawn	0	1	2	3	5	
I rake the lawn	0	1	2	3	5	
I prune or trim the trees/shrubs/hedges	0	1	2	3	5	
I plant and care for our flowerbeds	0	1	2	3	5	
I de-litter the grounds	0	1	2	3	5	
I keep all paths and drives swept	0	1	2	3	5	
I clean out the garage	0	1	2	3	5	
VEHICLES						
I clean the inside of the car	0	1	2	3	5	
I wash the outside of the car	0	1	2	3	5	
I make sure the car has petrol after I've used it	0	1	2	3	5	
I arrange for repairs and servicing	0	1	2	3	5	
I check and maintain oil, water and other fluid levels	0	1	2	3	5	
MISCELLANEOUS						
I run my own errands	0	1	2	3	5	
I wait at home for the plumber, electrician, gas man, etc.	0	1	2	3	5	

	Never	Once in a While	50% of the Time	Most of the Time	Always	Score
I pack my own suitcases	0	1	2	3	5	
I feed and clean up after my/our pets	0	1	2	3	5	
If there's a problem at home I stay at home	0	1	2	3	5	
I hire cleaning help when we need it	0	1	2	3	5	
I make my own dental/medical/etc., appointments	0	1	2	3	5	

Rate yourself

Cad (0-25)

Egads, you cad! This book is probably your only hope of regaining the respect of the female species. Maybe you'd better read it twice.

Underachiever (25-75)

There's hope for you. Read the book before the end of the week. Once you apply what you've learned, you'll glow with self-esteem and other satisfactions ... I PROMISE!

Above Average (75-120)

Nothing to brag about, but you're definitely above the average inconsiderate man. A careful study of these pages should bring you the rest of the way up to scratch.

Macho Man (120-160)

Your example is invaluable. But do read all the way to the end to make sure there's nothing holding you back from absolute, total, amazing PERFECTION. And buy a copy as a gift for a worthless son-in-law or friend.

King Cleaner (160-390)

You're a liar! Go back and admit all the times you fudged the frequency of your contributions and adjust your score accordingly.

Chapter Three

No more feeble excuses

We males do some of our most creative thinking when we're trying to get out of household chores. I know *you* wouldn't do it, but you probably have a friend or two who would be shameless enough to fall back on one or more of the following:

It's a woman's job to clean ...
Anyone using this oldest of all excuses has got a screw loose. Anyone old enough to make a mess is old enough to clean a mess – and that means both sexes.

I haven't washed a plate in fifteen years
But you've dirtied more than twenty-five thousand – is that fair?

I'm the one who runs things in my house
YES, but you might try running things <u>around</u> the house for a change

– things like the vacuum cleaner, the washer, the floor mop, etc. ...

My mother always ...
She might be willing to take you back.

I have to be careful with my back/ dicky knee
It worked yesterday for squash and wrestling with the sons on the rug ... not to mention the mixed aerobics class.

I'm allergic to oven cleaner
Rubber gloves have more to offer than you ever imagined. (And you don't seem to have any problem with grease, oil, power-steering fluid, brake fluid, automatic-transmission fluid or windscreen washer.)

Only a sissy would clean ...
Some might think it's sissy to wear

designer cologne, flowered shirts or to have your hair styled, but how could it be sissy to learn to be a rugged, responsible cleaning professional? An apron might be the sexiest piece of apparel you ever wore!

The lads would laugh at me (I'd never live it down)
Would you ever live it down if your wife left you for a man who does wash up?

No time! I've got a pile of office work to do ...
You didn't even have ounces of office work to do during the world snooker or the Wimbledon finals.

I wouldn't know where to start
A simple 'Yes' would be wonderful.

Mañana ....

Why can't the kids help?
They can, they just need an example to see how it's done.

It doesn't need doing yet
Haven't you heard? Preventive maintenance is in.

I'd just botch it up if I did it anyway
Only practice makes perfect.

I don't do ...
Good for you. But what if she said that about the cooking?

I do the outdoor work
Maybe you should move into the garden.

With a degree in theoretical physics, you expect me to do manual work?
Living is a hands-on profession, and the challenges of housework should be a doddle for a mind like yours.

The game is on ...
Well, the soup isn't and won't be until the shopping's done.

I'll do it when I feel like it ...
How do you feel when you wear dirty socks or a creased shirt?

You're better at it
I bet you could give her some stiff competition if you tried.

I already do a hard week's work
That didn't stop you from driving to Epsom on Derby Day.

It's my day off ...
Tell the nappies that.

What do you think I married you for?
She's probably asking the same question.

I don't mind a mess
Is that why you keep making them?

It doesn't look bad
That's what you said just before the water heater exploded.

If I put it away, I won't be able to find it when I need it
Can you find it now?

If you didn't nag me all the time, I'd do it
She didn't nag you for the first ten years – and you never did it.

I don't know how ...
Neither did she when she started. Now that you're admitting you need to know how to jump up and do it, read Chapter 6 of this book or get "Is There Life After Housework?" and you'll know more about cleaning than fifty per cent of the people running around with a cleaner's uniform on.

Just leave it to me ... I'll take care of it
"Leave it" is the key phrase here.

By now you can work out the answer to the rest of these:
You weren't out long enough."

"I've got to help Stan move his stuffed fish."

"You can't do that in this kind of weather." (It's too hot, too cold, too windy, too humid, too dry, it might rain, snow, sleet or hail.)

"The (lawnmower, strimmer, chain saw, drill, paint sprayer, etc.) needs looking at before I can do that.

"I have to have a sleep first."

"I'll do it later."

"I'll do that during my holiday."

"I'll do it as soon as I get back from the pub."

Chapter Four

Yes you can do it!

The helpless Harry act

It's masculine to be handy, but smarter to be unhandy. The "unhandy" man can escape all manner of make-it and fix-it jobs.

Women believe it, too. They've been brainwashed by all those cartoons showing the man of the house up to his neck in water trying to fix the plumbing, or some electrical engineer reading the Christmas toy assembly directions upside down. Or he studiously examines the broken or out-of-adjustment item and in a trial-lawyer voice says, "Mmmm ... I don't have the right metric tool for this" or "we need a part from Japan." Most women won't question tools or parts and the hunk of an unhandy husband slithers out of mending things. And if all else fails, a despairing fling of the screwdriver will make any woman back off.

But there is absolutely no such thing as being unhandy at *housework.* Some men may have electrical, mechanical or mathematical limitations, but there need be no housework hesitations. Anyone who can walk and smoke a cigarette at the same time can keep a home spotless. If you can wash your hands, you can wash anything. If you can polish a hubcap, you can polish a sink. And even if you can't pick up a tennis ball on your racket you can pick up a shoe.

Hairy-chested housework

Would you believe that *elevation* even affects the housework we men are willing to do? Here is some scientific proof.

Somehow country air cures all housework apprehensions. We will

45

tiptoe past simple housework duties at home, then stampede into the country and do every housework task in its most ghastly primitive state. We won't touch a dish, pan, packet or washing machine at home and we turn up our noses at a less-than-perfectly cooked egg. Yet hours later, in our rustic campsite, we will (fighting wind, ants, midges or freezing temperatures) over a fire we had to collect wood for and build, reduce an innocent egg to a charred blob and happily eat it cold. We permanently blacken the virtue of spotless pans and kettles, while getting smoked, scorched and grease-burned ourselves. We uncomplainingly wash our clothes by hand in a cold stream and laboriously brush out the tent with a pine branch. We even make our bed fastidiously (roll up our sleeping bag and perform the gymnastics necessary to get it back into its sack). And get this: we pack all these housework supplies on our backs so we can be *sure* we will be able to do it ... and we even *pay* willingly and generously so we can do all this.

What could be more manly than being fair and consistent? Home housework is not only ten times easier and more convenient to do, it's more impressive and appreciated than the most hairy-chested heroics. Be a real hero, carry your campfire consciousness back to the kitchen.

Sit down and keep quiet! This is man's work!

Military manoeuvres ... on the home front

I know for a fact those of you who've been in the armed forces know how to clean. You *had* to know, just to survive. You not only learned to cope with keep fit, to fit everything into a footlocker and to keep everything in its place, but you even cleaned well enough to pass that dreaded *weekly inspection.* Your bed had to be made so taut a penny would bounce off it; uniforms had to be knife-edge pressed; blankets had to be folded so that no edges showed; and you know well what it is to fall out of the barracks and police the area. Now that the Sergeant Major isn't glaring down at you, you've simply slackened off. More likely than not, you're just out of the habit of doing things regularly and keeping things tidy. Let's revive those spit and polish skills and use them on the home front.

We can do it ... because we *do* do it

Consider the fact that eighty per cent of all the professional cleaning companies in the world are owned and operated by men, and of the cleaning chores they undertake to do, seventy per cent are performed by men. Commercial cleaning is no different from the home type, except that commercial cleaning is actually harder – since

Not there! That's the mug branch!

it involves more square feet and heavier machinery.

Men learn faster!

Speaking as someone who's trained and employed tens of thousands of cleaning employees in homes and commercial establishments, I can tell you that men very often catch on faster and work faster than women ... even cleaning the delicate goods. Once, for example, I was called to do a large job where a basement fire had left a couple's home smoke-stained and damaged. You're not going to believe this, but they had (it was recorded on the insurance proof of loss) seven thousand, two hundred individual figurines and shelved pieces of rare and unusual ornaments.

Thinking like the average man, I thought this painstaking task had to be a woman's job, so I hired a group of women. They were slow – not as familiar with the mechanics of production, perhaps, as were my regular cleaning team, who were not only faster, but neater than their female counterparts.

We're simply better at it.

Most housework jobs are mechanical, and men are generally more at home with such chores than women. That's not just hearsay, it's a scientific fact. When you look at the nature of the operations involved in cleaning, and the equipment and supplies needed to do it – it's amazing that it was ever assigned to women in the first place.

Housework is tough, demanding, sometimes dangerous work that takes both skill and stamina.

As far as skill goes, no woman will ever be able to clean as well and as fast as a man. Men are more adept at manipulating objects (like mops and buckets), and they're taller, so they can reach high shelves in a single bound. They're stronger, so they can muscle those obstructions out of the way and lift and heave with ease. Their longer arms and strong hands can easily reach the spot near the top, and they can climb more easily up the ladder to wash the ceiling or the walls. They excel at practical problem-solving, which housework abounds in, and are far less likely to cringe at the sight of a spider or silverfish.

So you see, physically and emotionally, men are better suited to the basic requirements of cleaning (eat your heart out, you females). On average, women are more meticulous and a little more consistent, but I believe this is not an inborn physical or mental trait; simply the habit of commitment they have towards the job. As I and my crew of professional cleaners attacked hundreds of homes to clean them over the years, the women owners of the homes actually felt more confident when a male crew was working. Look around at who's cleaning our modern tower blocks; women don't dominate the cleaning kingdom at work – why should they at home?

Your share ... even Steven

There are many different time zones in the world. These are mostly very precise and accurate; only one is totally unpredictable and utterly erratic and that is the "last time" you did something.

We men think we help more than we do. Man after man (even ministers and youth leaders) will tell me in all sincerity and apparent honesty that they help around the house. Yet not one of them can tell me where the cleaning stuff is, or how to use it. Most can't get the new safety lids off, so that tells you something about when "the last time" was. Last times in cleaning are like when you last phoned a friend, went to the dentist or had a medical. It wasn't days, weeks, or even months ... but always *years* ago.

I read volumes and articles of theory and instuction about *how* and *why* to divide up the cleaning so everyone has his and her fair share. Get the word "share" out of your voc-

abulary. Thousands of words and little messages and lists have been written to get people to do their share of something. Splitting anything is always a risky business. No one – bank robbers, business partners, sales people, etc. – is at their best when it's time to divide the loot or the assignment.

In the housework arena, if you're worrying about each doing his or her exact share, forget it. We don't split work and *expect* each other to do his or her share – we both work together to get it done. Whoever finishes first helps the other so they can get it all done faster and do something else together. Everyone does all he or she can in the time they can spare.

The cure to the "housework" problem will come from one basic thing: each of us being aware and considerate enough to take care of our own junk and mess, and being willing to pitch in once in a while with someone else's mess. It doesn't matter who did it last time; all that counts is that we end up with and enjoy a clean, neat setting – so just jump in and do it. *Don't keep the score!*

And don't kid yourself. There's a big difference between *helping* and *doing*. For example, feeding the family – the never-ending job. A friend once said, "I take care of the food. I do the shopping."

Was he off his head! Taking care of the food means:

I think it's your turn, dearest!

> Planning the menu
>
> Listing the ingredients needed
>
> Picking them out (or finding them) at the supermarket
>
> Bringing them home
>
> Putting them away
>
> Preparing them (washing, peeling, chopping, tenderizing, etc.)

Cooking

Setting and decorating the table

Serving the meal

Eating

Wiping up spills

Clearing the table

Cleaning the kitchen and eating area

Washing-up

Drying up

Putting everything away

Freezing and preserving

Planning and giving parties, etc.

O.K., Maestro — when you're ready!

The man of the house is often involved in only one of these steps – the eating. (Even when he goes to the supermarket, he's not usually shopping, he's just following her list.) And though there are some men who cook, many others would only be caught with a pot in their hand at a cheese-and-wine party and other meals that involve an audience.

The same goes for the washing, of which some part must be done every day:

Gathering dirty clothes from the linen basket and elsewhere

Sorting

Pre-treating stains

Washing

Drying

Folding

Ironing

Putting away

Mending as needed

Taking clothes to the dry cleaner and picking them up

Skip – is that a squirrel or a hedgehog?

Take the initiative

A willingness to tackle something that needs to be done (without being asked or nagged) shows appreciation. "Can I help you?" is better than nothing, but it doesn't express full love and commitment; taking the initiative does. My wife taught me a startling lesson in this regard. When friends of the family lost their father, I tried to express my compassion and concern by asking, "Is there anything I can do?" "Oh ... no ... there's not much anyone can do now." My wife, however, knew something we all need to learn and practise: don't ask, *do*.

Barbara knew the whole family was coming to the home of the widow and things would be crowded. So she cleaned up our caravan, made up the beds and drove it over to their house and just left it there, so they couldn't refuse. Then she phoned and said, "The caravan is there, please use it." They loved it and they didn't have to ask.

We can't escape the law of carry-over

It may be hard to imagine, but the personal value of cleaning is great. Getting someone to clean up our mess is about as clever as having them exercise, eat and have sex for us. Cleaning up our own mess keeps us in touch with things as they really are. If we only went to the party and didn't ever help with the preparations or the cleaning up, we'd never see the foundation of effort and organization that underlies even the most carefree moments. If we don't ever do the washing or mop a floor, we won't understand that restoration is a very real part of use.

Cleaning up our own mess gets down to the heart of responsibility. What could be more basic than putting back in order the things we disordered, removing the dirt we ourselves trampled in?

Seventy per cent of housework is clutter and litter control, and the daily demands of dealing with the aftermath of eating, grooming, dressing. It's the clothes we wear, the food and paper we go through daily. That's why housework isn't a woman's or even a family's job, but a personal, individual responsibility.

The *biggest* reason women shouldn't have to do all the cleaning is the unspoken implication of that. It's in effect saying: *let somebody else do it.*

Every pattern and attitude we acquire in one area of our life carries over into other areas. If we dodge our chores as a child, we're likely to do the same in our marriage and our career. If we grow up wasting things, we may well be wasteful of time and life later. The youngster who drops out of the leaf raking team will probably be the one who drops out of the sales analysis team at work. People who never learned to see a mess around them won't recognize a problem when it happens in their business, health or marriage.

If we learn at home (where we spend most of our time) to be unresponsive to commitments and promises, if we live at home insensitive to others' needs, we'll carry it right along with us to the outside world.

As I write this in a large scout camp dining hall, the head of the camp came in, plugged his razor in the socket on the centre pole between tables, shaved with an electric razor, then took the razor head off and blew whiskers all over the tables and clean floor.

If we only did housework for one reason – the incalculable value of carry-over – it would be worth it.

Your Mum needs a break, son – why don't you get yourself a wife?

Twelve reasons to hog the housework

1   **Peace and a clear conscience**
No more wasted time, no more mental anguish – dodging, sneaking, excuse-making, debating – no more nagging, bargaining, complaining, bitching, questioning, no more fights. Facing up to a few minutes of housework is much easier than haggling and scheming. Simply *doing* some housework is the easy way out.

2   **How could you reap bigger benefits from just a few minutes a day?**
Doing your share plus a little extra will probably take about twenty minutes a day, maybe an hour or two on Saturday. Where can you find time for housework in your hectic life? What about the time you spend

re-reading the sports page, evaluating your neighbour's progress on his new patio while you have another cup of coffee, or watching some idiot programme on TV? Think for a minute – which will have the most dramatic effect on your life and home circumstances? It's an easy answer: *jump at the housework.*

3   **Exercise**
Why waste your time riding stationary bicycles or wrestling on the floor with expensive muscle-building contraptions? Cleaning is the perfect exercise – just enough running up the stairs or lifting, bending and reaching to keep the old body in shape. Look around you (maybe even at you) – at

55

all the men who are getting pot bellies and looking like waddling pears. Housework is exercise with a purpose, as well as a reward. Name any other exercise you can get (unless you're lucky enough to live on a farm) so conveniently.

4 Good clean therapy

Irritated, agitated, pent up, tense? Try a spot of housework. What a chance to unwind and put your body to work while your mind works out the frustrations (and maybe even the problem itself). There's something about improving a dirty condition that also improves our mental condition; the act of cleaning has an oddly soothing and purifying effect. And as women have known for centuries, there's hardly a better or more productive way to work off guilt, anger and aggravation.

5 You'll get real *satisfaction* from it

After a day of shuffling papers and attending meetings, soldering circuits on the production line, being hassled by the regional manager or coping with the complaints of customers, you'll find the genuine *immediate* pleasure you get from looking at a freshly vacuumed floor or a

I cleaned up!

newly washed window a refreshing change and a real thrill. You can see, feel, really *tell* what you did today. There's an undeniable satisfaction that comes with restoring order, with getting it all together. And dealing with long overdue things banishes guilt. In fact, the dirtier and messier things are, the better you'll feel when you're finished.

Besides, it's great to come from a difficult day to a clean home. All your senses have something to rejoice in, and the order that meets your eye when you open the door will fill you with a calm, restful feeling. You'll find immense satisfaction in knowing *you* created all this.

6 You'll learn the real survival skills of modern life

Forget those expensive courses in surviving desert disasters or Himalayan hardship. Unless you're rich, unemployed or extraordinarily unlucky you have about a one-in-a hundred thousand chance of ever putting them to use. But knowing how to take care of yourself in your everyday environment is a skill *nobody* should be without.

We all have to manage on our own sometimes and these days we're all single longer – and more often. The man of the John Wayne generation who learns to clean won't ever have to marry just to have someone to keep house. And you men of the future *have* to know how to do it. The new crop of women growing up isn't going to do it all quietly, automatically and uncomplainingly any more. Besides, it'll make you more capable of attracting a dynamic mate.

7 At last, you have a chance to get things the way you really like them

You're the one who wants the living room to always look presentable? Do you hate to see dishes left in the sink? And you *despise* the idea of somebody else messing about with your stuff? Here's your big chance to "have it your way". You can help ensure that your home is as clean, comfortable and orderly as *you* want it to be, and not just the way your mate happens to want things or is able to manage to keep things.

8 It's a whole new chance to brag and show off

Forget that tired old talk of how many miles you ran or how you landed that monster trout. When you start reeling off those statistics of how many tile joints you whitened and cookers you decrusted, your pals will be utterly speechless. This is a real growth area for one-upmanship.

9 You'll save money

Keeping things tidied away keeps them from depreciating, rotting, breaking, getting stolen, rained on, etc. Carpets, curtains, furniture, all last longer if cleaned and maintained regularly – some things will last twice as long. Imagine replacing fitted carpets every fifteen years instead of every six – what you save could pay for a home computer or a VCR. You'll also save using professional cleaners; they cost money, and there's nothing they do that you can't; I promise you this is true.

10 Women become warm and playful when ...

The house is clean, organised and running smoothly. Take over some of the work and you'll have more time to play together. She'll be less irritated, less naggy, prettier, a little more likely to believe that you really do *care* ... and you can use your imagination from there. We'll really make all those macho foreign lovers sweat when we start making housework a home grown passion.

11 A chance to set a good example

Someone in the family, some time, is going to have to break the tradition

that it's the mother's and daughters' job to clean, cook, wash, etc. Before you launch into the old trap of "share and assign" a regimented family cleaning programme, remember that around the house *example* from the father is a lot more effective than rules pinned on a notice board. You don't need to give stirring speeches; just the simple act of *doing* some housework, without being asked, will do much more to change the lives of family members. Example is still the very best – if not the *only* – effective way to teach anything. It's the quickest, easiest, surest way to change attitudes and behaviour patterns.

We men don't spend much time reaching and teaching our children; by doing the cleaning we are a living example going through the house. Housework is one of the few handy opportunities we have to gain our children's respect, show them how to be loving, thoughtful beings. Don't let it escape.

12 You could make a career of it

(And you'll be trained for another profession when your unemployment day arrives).

I became a millionaire doing housework, and all the time I've been free and independent, kept fit and had the chance to travel the world and meet and enjoy tens of thousands of people. After you've learned to clean around the house and you've got your home in order, you might want to think about doing it full- or part-time (or as a family) for a living.

You won't even have to clean under your fingernails; you can thumb your nose at all your high-powered relatives. And as you learn and grow, you'll want to find a way to do it faster and better like our brilliant species always does. You might even invent new tools and procedures and become rich and famous in the process.

Chapter Five

What can you do to help?

Did you ever step on a rake you forgot to pick up and get a punctured foot? Or have the handle give you a black eye? Ever find your pliers by sitting down on them, or back the car over something you popped down and left there? Ever need something in an emergency, and not been able to use it because you didn't put it back or fix it when you had it out last?

These are just a few little examples of the kinds of problems we inflict upon ourselves through neglect and thoughtlessness. Imagine what these and similar habits do to *others* in our homes, offices or organizations.

I heard this comment once and thought it summarized the situation well: a non-housecleaning husband said to his wife on Mother's Day,

"Dear, is there any way that I can help you with the housework?" Her reply,"Dear, if you just clean up all of your own things there won't *be* any housework."

Examine your own conduct. It will be a revelation to you. Picking up and cleaning up after yourself will be the single most useful thing you can do. It's much more pleasant, easier and safer to work in orderly surroundings. It took me a while but I finally discovered that if I put my spanners away, my DIY goods away, my fishing tackle away, my squash gear away, when it was time to work or play I could do it straightaway. I didn't have to hunt and rummage.

Remember: There's nothing wrong with making a mess, that's often progress in the works. It's leaving it that is wrong.

In short:

If you open it, close it

If you turn it on, turn it off

If you unlock it, lock it

If you break it, fix it

If you can't fix it, throw it away

If you borrow it, return it

If you make a mess, clean it up

If you've finished with it, put it back

If you don't know where it goes – ASK!

We can be our own buzzards.

When new territories were being won, if a horse was injured or a wagon

ruined, our rough, tough forebears shot the horse where it fell or the wagon was pushed over a cliff. Expired or exhausted things were thrown away and left along the trail for the buzzards. We rugged males today are exactly the same. We can round up, find, prepare and carry something fifty miles to use it, but we can't seem to make it fifty feet to get rid of it or put it away when we're finished.

We seem especially incapable of disposing of anything empty (cans, bottles, jars, boxes). We finish it off, but almost *never* go any further. And when something stops working (mower, cultivator, drill, etc.), isn't it amazing how the thing is instantly immobile? Machines, motors, even vehicles – we leave them right where they died. So we stumble over them as well as clutter up the place. It must be because we have a subconscious assurance that The Great Gatherer (a woman) will come along and pick it up for us.

Women shouldn't have to be our buzzards. If we're man enough to crush a can with one mighty squeeze, we ought to be able to toss it in the rubbish bin.

The manly art of flinging

We males undoubtedly have an uncanny knack for "distributing" things.

My dad once asked me to pick up a "hand broadcaster" at the hardware shop. I gave him a puzzled look and he said, "It's a machine you put stuff in, turn a handle, and it throws the stuff all over the place." Sound like a quick description of a man? The minute we turn the door handle of the house, we begin to "broadcast" things.

We start by tracking dirt in on our boots. We think being engrossed in an important project justifies not cleaning the grease off our hands. (In fact, we're a little proud of it.) Thus everything we touch is marked; we even throw our oily overalls on top of "clean" laundry. When (if) we do wash our hands, we leave the sink and everything else in the bathroom dirtier than we were. And guess who leaves those black heel marks on the clean kitchen floor?

We frown if a piece of peel is left on the work surface, yet we always leave shavings, sawdust, filings, behind. It's everywhere! The only time our gloves aren't flung somewhere is when we're wearing them. Most of us really believe the second purpose of socks and shoes is to test the agility of women's pick-up power. I bet that if there weren't women nurses cleaning up after male doctors, there would be livers, gizzards and gallstones knee-deep in the surgery.

In my nearly fifty years I've walked

62

... and that is the end of the news!

in the door after work as a manure-footed farmer, a grease-coated mechanic, a paint-spattered professional painter, a dusty contractor and a paper-scattering student. As I reflect on the reason for this thoughtlessness, I remember that even as a youth on the farm, the trampling in of straw or mud by men was tolerated because it was "work dirt". Who – especially a *woman* – would dare question the sanctity of work dirt? It was as hallowed as a battle scar.

The cause doesn't justify the mess. *Don't put it down – put it away!*

We know that a real man takes care of his own responsibilities. Our own daily personal mess should be Number 1. Who would be thoughtless enough to make another person clean up his leftovers and bits and pieces? Not a *man*, I hope!

Men, here are the BIG TEN

1 Clothes clobber

Your sole responsibility to clothes is not just wearing them, as has been supposed for at least eight thousand years. Caring for them – picking them up, hanging them up, folding them – cleaning and disposing of them when necessary are part of the picture, too. We value our clothes for comfort, image, looks – who should be more concerned with their maintenance, preservation and accessibility than us?

2 Food mess

The issue of dishes is covered in Chapter 6. The very *least* we can do is to not leave food container lids off, packets undone, empty food and drink containers and wrappers lying around.

3 Project debris

Have we ever cleaned up after our wife or daughter's craft or school projects? *Never!* Have they ever cleaned up ours ...? The fact that we do a giant project doesn't give us immunity from cleaning up: sawdust, solder, wood shavings, plaster dust, etc. We don't have to leave a mess in plain view to advertise our accomplishments. What we actually did accomplish will be appreciated even *more* if it doesn't leave a giant cleaning-up job behind.

4 Sports mess

We men play golf, squash, football or whatever and think our activity is over when the game ends. We lay muddy boots, smelly bait, sweaty shirts, soggy towels and racquets all over the living room and finally end up asking the wife when she is going to cook that smelly unappetizing fish. Real sports put their sports stuff away after using it ... and gut their own fish!

5 Junk

Women are equally guilty of this, of course, but I'd like to note here that we men do have our very own entirely masculine species of junk and clutter (which can be loosely defined as things we don't really want or need, but we keep around to bung up our storage space, worry and distract us). Raise your clutter consciousness today – see p. 69 to 72 – and put that throwing arm in action, brother!

6 Drawer/cupboard mess

These are storage places, not directions to sling things in or hidden clutter bins. Keep drawers closed and tidy.

7 Paper paraphernalia

Magazines, newspapers, junk mail and other mail is shamelessly piled and accumulated by the majority of us men, waiting for the woman or the cleaner to throw it away. How are they supposed to know whether it's important, whether we're finished with it or not, what we want to save, etc.? Let's take care of *all* our own paper products.

8 Smoking residue

Cleaning up afer smoking is, all in all, almost as time-consuming as cleaning up after eating. It isn't just those overflowing (and spilled) ashtrays and half-used match boxes everywhere, it's the dropped butts and ashes flicked onto floors, into sinks, and even houseplants. It's holes burned in tablecloths, burn marks on coasters and plastic fixtures, and a nasty smell that permeates clothes, furniture, car interiors and even pets; not to mention the tar deposits and yellow stain on every wall, window and ceiling surface. If you won't stop, you can at least help with the cleaning up.

9 Pet problems

Animals can be fun to have around, but when it comes to the incidentals such as feeding, watering, kennel cleaning, trips to the vet, walking, bathing, brushing, cleaning up hair and repairing chewed furniture, "man's best friend" is usually tended by woman (see p. 73).

10 Bathroom beastliness

The returns are in, and they overwhelmingly indict the bathroom as a trouble spot. In the time we men spend there we manage to leave all manner of mess and unsightly evidence of our presence. A little forethought here will go a long way.

Food fallout

We all have our own candidates for Number 1 mess, but food mess is undoubtedly a biggie. Dirty dishes three times a day is enough to drive any person to the brink, but when you add in-between meals and late-night snacks, it's like dumping a bucket of dirty mop water on your wife's head. I can remember the days when at about four in the afernoon we children would rip into the bread and peanut butter and jam for a snack to tide us over ... and always leave the jars open, crumbs everywhere and the sticky utensils on the worktop. We tided ourselves over – but we didn't tidy up the kitchen.

Most men leave snacks or short meals and food and tea break residue where they finish ... which is no better than a feedlot pig does. The two-minute job of cleaning up is now a ten-minute job for the woman. There is no excuse for this – none. It was our snack, our mess, our stomach.

Some food foibles to be avoided

Grotty growths Taking cups of coffee, bowls of soup, ham sandwiches – whatever happens to be on today's menu – into the shop, shed or spare room, and leaving behind what will become an encrusted plate, mouldy cup or scummy bowl.

Shell-shock Leaving shells, peels and empty packets behind wherever we happen to be eating peanuts, oranges or potato crisps. (I hope we all know better than to eat biscuits in bed).

Wrap it up Putting cheese, meat, etc., back into the fridge unwrapped; putting jars, bottles, etc., back without their tops or caps on. (This doesn't mean close it and put it back for others to scrape out if there is only a tiny bit left.

Sour stuff Drinking directly from the milk bottle or fruit juice carton, leaving the milk or butter out on the worktop.

Unremovable rings Putting wet glasses on wooden furniture without coasters, which leaves an ugly (and hard if not impossible to remove) white ring.

Out of ice again Don't leave the empty ice-cube tray lying around – rinse and refill, it and put it back to freeze.

Move it When you push, squeeze or jam left-overs into an already-full refrigerator, something's bound to get spilt. Look for wasted space or food that's gone off that can be thrown out to make room.

Bacon snitching and other piggies If you scoff all the mozzarella at midnight, how's she going to make the lasagna? Ask before you eat it – if it's clearly not a normal inhabitant of the refrigerator. Freezer raiding is even more insidious, because the theft isn't discovered until it's too late. You hardcore cases know who you are!

Strange brews and other unpleasant surprises Don't bung stuff you're hiding from the dog in the refrigerator. If you're undecided about something, throw it out now. And if you do put something awful in there (your ripened livers and bait for fishing, a five-pound sack of grass seed) admit your guilt before it ferments or sprouts and dispose of it.

Squatter's rights: table tops

Did you know burglars can rob a man's bedroom much faster and more efficiently than a woman's? To find a woman's treasures they have to get into drawers, search and dig. Bagging a man's valuables and mementos is a piece of cake. All they have to do is scoop it off the top of the bedside table. Table tops were never officially granted to either sex, but we men somehow assumed all this territory for our tools, receipts, pens, pencils, pocket-knives, cuff-links, loose change, golf tees, half-toothpicks, used hankies. When we put what we need back into our pockets in the morning, we leave the questionable things, hoping that a junk gremlin (or a woman!) will dispose of it. Let's start undressing the dressing table top!

Some wardrobe courtesies

We men blame all wardrobe mess on women, but we are just as rash and reckless with these storage spaces out of public sight. We, too, have a good part of our college clothes still secreted in there, along with our ancient football team uniform and the Hawaiian shirts, bush hat, ski gear and embroidered lederhosen we'll never wear. A two-foot thick anorak eats up an unholy chunk of "our space", and it stays there all year, not just during the three-month season in which we wear it at least twice. We'd have room for it, though, if we chucked out our complete historical collection of tie widths, baggy Irish jumpers and stained shirts.

To find the floor, we'd have to move a superstructure of bent and collapsed hangers, an assortment of jaded jogging shoes, and those good-as-new wellies that keep falling over. The snorkelling equipment we never use is what we'd find at the bottom.

The only things *not* in the wardrobe are our clean clothes (which are still downstairs waiting for a woman to reroute them, or draped on a doorknob, open drawer or banister somewhere).

A friend of mine said when she discovered that her new husband left his trousers on the floor where he took them off, she kicked them under the bed. Two days later he left his work trousers in the same place and she kicked *them* under the bed. After she repeated this ritual with seven pairs of trousers, the new husband's wardrobe was depleted. He came into the kitchen wrapped in a towel, saying, "Darling, do you know where all my trousers are?"

"Yes. Under the bed right where you left them." For the next forty

The first thing you'll need, son, is a junk bench...

years of marriage and to this day, he's never left his trousers to be picked up.

In case you wondered.

Throw	*really means*	hang
Cram	*really means*	fold
Pile	*really means*	place
Keepable	*really means*	usable
Store	*really means*	trash

Caution: men at work

There is no more impressive male territorial intimidator than the workbench. It's far more forbidden territory than a woman's sewing room is to a man. All of those tools and power gadgets, the "keep away" smells of unfamiliar solvents, all those gauges, testers and sharpeners are, by their very nature, a keep-out sign to the female. They make her feel unworthy to consider any encroachment on or to question any expansion of the area.

In reality, a lot of the apparatus in a workshop is about as hard to operate as the electric can opener in the kitchen. Isn't it amazing that for all the room it takes up, all the elaborate equipment and accessories, investment and insurance, how little ever comes out of it? I bet more actual mending and parts and tools come out of the kitchen "junk" drawer than many an entire workshop.

What actually inhabits the workshop, for the most part?

important fluids in rusty tins with no labels

oily rags

dead batteries

stray blobs of solder

holey hosepipe

dried-up tins of left-over paint

petrified paintbrushes

coffee jars half full of unidentifiable objects

unsorted nails, rusty screws and washers in everything but the size you need

broken parts

obsolete plumbing fittings and unreliable electrical parts

dead machines

old number plates and hubcaps

greasy unread back issues of car magazines

These things aren't just fire hazards, they're ugly and smelly. Convert the junk bench back to a workbench!

Junk knows no gender

We men are astonishing hoarders and our junk takes up much more than its share of the room. We have stuff stored away we can't remember and that we'll never use again. All sorts

It's confetti – you never know when it might come in useful...

of things. You would weep if you knew how many of your wives have phoned and written to me to pour their hearts out about your clobber ... Every note you ever took in medical school, three classic cars (none of which go), twenty-five years' worth of *Amateur Photographer* (plus unused dark-room to match), your great-grandfather's lawn bowling trophies, a guitar with two strings, expensive (and ugly) collector's decanters, luckless lottery tickets, dusty and dismembered radios and TVs, school magazines you haven't looked at in thirty years, the stamp collection you were very keen on in the fifth form, the wreckage of your model of the *Santa Maria,* elaborate equipment for a succession of hobbies you've lost interest in or never got around to and at least half-a-pound of unidentified keys.

Clear everything out and don't worry if your wife happens to be a bigger rubbish hoarder than you – we all think that. The best way to get her to throw out her clutter is by leadership and example. "Hey, look, Joan, I've tidied up and I'm free." Jump up and click your heels – and watch her tackle her piles of rubbish.

When you've been through your cupboards, drawers, den and glove compartment and that cave of clutter known as the garage, you can move on to:

The attic, cellar and like storage areas

These are always creepy and crawly and filled with heavy, bulky, ancient things. About seventy-five per cent of this "treasure" is junk – not to mention booby traps and fire hazards – so you can safely assume the aggressor role of grubbing and grabbing all the dead-end entities in and around these places. She can't do it or she won't (mainly because most of it is *yours* so she can't decide). Right now, burrow in and mark and murder the junk.

Throw out the rubbish and give anything good to the charity of your choice. If you can't bear to part with something, put it in an "emotional

Don't just stand there

withdrawal" box and seal it. Three weeks later, you can throw the box out (you won't remember what's in there, so it won't hurt a bit).

Pet peeves

Pets have the distinction of joint ownership, but seldom joint cleanership. When you remove *di* and *tion* from distinction, what do you have left?

Pet care involves a lot more than footing the grub and vet's bill. Those lovable creatures, while spreading joy, also spread hair (and often worse until they're house trained). Who do you usually find feeding, grooming, exercising and cleaning up after an animal? Who empties the litter box, takes the pet for its jabs? That's right, the woman. It's always *our* dog at a show, hers when it smells after getting into the compost heap. The cat is hers when it moults and scratches, ours when it's looking for a lap to purr in. Men have always found it more macho to horse around than to actually lead the horse to water (and then stand and wait while it delicately sips ten endless gallons). About the only thing we take the initiative in here is teaching pets bad habits – such as licking dishes or leaping onto the bed or the furniture.

And yet, from Adam's very first instructions, animal care was a *masculine* tradition. Miraculous, isn't it (not to mention convenient) how evolution has again occurred. Don't let your wife and children get stuck with all the dirty work.

— fetch the dog!

Fetch, female!

"Fetch" ... was all we had to yell as youngsters when we wanted something and there was a beloved mum or little sister who enthusiastically dug it out and brought it to us. Later, we only had to throw a stick from the bank and our faithful dog jumped into the icy water to bring it to our feet. In time, we assumed that all we had to do was whistle and someone would jump. Finding "fetch" a magic word, most of us then replaced Mother and Rover with a wife.

Knowing (if not appreciating) the value of a fetching female, we've even mastered the art of subconscious suggestion, or camouflaged "Fetch". By indirect, implied means we can still bellow for her to fetch:

"While you're up, I wouldn't mind another cup of coffee."

"I think I will have a piece of pie now."

"We don't seem to have enough serviettes ..."

"Have you seen my shoes?"

"Isn't there anything better on the other channel?"

"Where are my clean shirts?"

"Where did I put my keys?"

"Where did you hide the scissors?"

"It's time to feed Fido."

"How about a sandwich?"

"Aren't there any biscuits?"

"I think the fire is going out ..."

"We're out of toilet paper again?"

Run your own errands (for a change)

Like most of you I am always trying to do five things more than I can achieve and always need something now or yesterday that I was too busy to get, or too lazy to think of before now. Inevitably, when that pressing need arises, I never consider doing the errand myself but call out for someone else to run and get it. In essence saying, "I'm too busy and important to waste time on something like this."

I was forty-eight before I suddenly realized how many times I had unthinkingly and unappreciatively yelled "fetch" to my wife and children. _

At that point, with eight teenagers and a thriving business, I had eight home and farm vehicles and forty company vehicles. When the road tax was about to expire, I'd holler for help, generally at the last minute, and my wife would head for the post office. Soon, as if by magic, a crisp current tax disc would appear on my desk. This system worked beautifully for twenty years, until my wife happened to be visiting a daughter and her new baby at renewal time. So I decided to take care of this little detail myself. I dug the registration document out of the glove compartment and zoomed to the post office ... where there was a ghastly queue. I stood in it, being elbowed and crowded with all the other wives – ten minutes, twenty minutes, forty minutes, an hour. Children were screaming and kept dripping ice cream on my new suit. A wheezing pot-bellied man behind me smoked about four hundred cigarettes, people were coughing, grumbling, swearing on all sides.

When I got to the clerk, I couldn't get the tax disc after all because I'd forgotten to bring the insurance certificate. The clerk muttered under her breath, "Should have sent your wife."

I was emotionally wounded by the experience and later asked my wife if it was that bad all the time. "An hour is *good* time," she said. For twenty years, for fleets of cars, I'd sent her to get my tax. How could I have been that inconsiderate? It's easy when you've been conditioned all your life to think that it's a woman's job to fetch. I'd never thanked her once!

The phrase "errand boy" is one of the most ironic errors of our vocabulary. Most, if not all, errands are run by the *women* of the world. Just tell me who runs ninety per cent of your errands – your wife, one of the children, your secretary. Even if you're handier and have the time, you won't do it; you'll come all the way home or get to the office and then send them forth. "Would you pick up some ..." "While you're in town, Dear, get me a ..." "I'm going to need .... for the board meeting tomorrow. Would you mind ..."

Errands are a sacrifice of time and life. Errands take time, errands mean getting stuck in the traffic, queues, busy telephones, indifferent or intimidating salespeople, postal delays, wild goose chases.

It is *not* a privilege for someone to spend her life and time on our behalf – yet "pick this or that up for me" is an automatic reflex for most men. You may pay someone to run business errands and that is fine, but at home, no one works for you, you work together. Programming a *please* in there would help – but not half as much as running our *own* errands at least part of the time.

If you suddenly ran all your own errands it would certainly cause heart failure, so take it easy and start by taking care of just a few. Then when your mate is adjusted to the shock, ask her occasionally if you can pick up something or run an errand for her. It'll take her a while to recover, but you'll be treated sweeter.

Surrender some unreasonable attitudes and demands ...

"We eat at exactly 6.00!"

"Not only the food but the plates will be warm!"

"Sheets are changed every other day, whether they need to be or not."

"I don't want to hear a peep out of the kids."

Just because your mother did it, the army insisted on it or you happen to be a prison warden doesn't mean the rules are right or necessary.

Where did we men learn to be "certified housework appraisers/evaluators" anyway? Certainly not from experience! My Aunt Glenda remarked, "Since we retired, after forty-five years of cleaning, I've found out I don't know how to sweep. My husband Jim now tells me I'm doing it all wrong." Our unreasonable attitudes and demands often have gestapo grimness. We don't give ourselves a certain time to do something or finish watching a game of football or fiddle with a new gadget – yet "she" better have "it" done on time.

What "our Mother did" loses authority with age; her floors, food, mending and organization were probably only about half as good as we now remember them. Yet these memories form our expectations of how things should be done in "our" present home. Expecting things to be just so when we come home from work or a game of golf with other 'business men' precludes the possibility that everything didn't go just right for her all day. Or that she may have been at work herself.

Chapter Six

House-cleaning crash course

At last. The course not taught at school or college, or even evening classes, a course that's required for intelligent and happy living. Though it has no grades, no tests and no attendance requirements it can make life more livable than ten terms of other courses combined.

In all of education today, the cry is "Back to the basics". What could be more basic than keeping the things we have to use and look at every day clean and pleasant to have around?

Forgive me if these basic housekeeping instructions insult your intelligence here and there. "I don't know how" keeps cropping up when household chores are involved. In this chapter I've tried to include all the gory details so "I don't know

how" won't stand in our way any more.

Tidying up

Professional cleaners and soldiers call this most basic of all cleaning operations "policing the area". It's a simple matter, when passing through an area, of slowing down enough to put a few items back in order. It takes no tools or no special skills – just an observant eye and a bend of the back and knees. The average home needs to be tidied up far more often than it needs to be cleaned, so this is a talent well worth cultivating. Any homemaker will tell you that tidying up and putting things away takes the most time of all.

Unfortunately, most of us men outgrew the urge to be policemen by the age of ten. When the fair sex straightened our tie before Sunday School, we took that as an eternal

commitment to straighten up everything for us. But the Sunday School truth is that "Anyone old enough to make a mess is old enough to clean it up." Indeed, brethren, in this case a helping hand beats a praying limb every time.

Tackling the Tenth-Time Offenders

We men are in an especially good position to do something about the repeat offenders, the things that have to be straightened up again and again and again. I'm talking about the things that are always a mess, that we seldom noticed or worried about before, because we were doing the messing up, not the straightening up. After you've rounded up scattered magazines for the twenty-ninth straight day, or raked up the droppings from the Mucho Sheddus Leafus plant, or retilted a tipped-over tray, you can take the initiative and

say, "How are we going to deal with this?" A high percentage of litter is caused by lack of official places to park things – lack of racks, hangers, hooks, shelves, cupboards, etc. A lot of things are like little tumbleweeds or third wheels loose in the house – always lying or drifting around somewhere. We can be eternal straighteners or straighten them up in one fell swoop, forever – send them up the river or down the chute. Why don't you suspend their licence to litter on your next policing patrol?

Anytime, anywhere you pass inches from a dropped newspaper, a crooked picture, an open drawer or door, a dead leaf, something spilled or wrinkled, something that needs to be tucked in, thrown out, adjusted, put back, *you can and should do it!* It only takes seconds and when done regularly saves a big cleaning binge. Fix it up, pick it up, straighten it, *straighten up* – it'll help you go straight in life!

Make your bed after you lie in it

Three years ago, I was amazed to realize that I'd slept in a bed eighteen thousand times in my lifetime – and probably only made a bed about 130 times. Who made all those beds? My wife? My daughters? The cleaning lady? When I thought about it, I had

80

to admit, in simple honest logic, that since I made at least half of it untidy every day, I should probably make it at least half the time.

I could understand a man shying away from "apron work" such as washing-up or doing the washing but a failure to pounce on the bed chores is unimaginable. Of all the places we should show respect if not *enthusiasm* for ... What provides the quality of experience, recreation and security a bed does? Let's get as serious about the after-care as the foreplay.

Changing the sheets

We'll start with this because changing the sheets is much more challenging than merely making the bed. When you change the sheets, do it like the hotel professionals – with a minimum of effort. They only walk around the bed *once*. (Unfortunately, this approach won't work with fitted sheets, which must be stretched from corner to corner of the mattress before the rest of the bed can be made.)

Stand by the bed and spread both top and bottom sheets across the mattress. Make sure they're smooth and straight. Next comes the blanket, then turn a few inches of the top sheet back and fold it over the blanket. Now, with everything shipshape, begin your circuit of the bed.

Starting at the headboard, tuck the sheet firmly beneath the mattress. (Hospital corners are stylish if you know how, but not necessary.) You're tucking in at least two layers – if there's a blanket, three – down one side and then around the bottom. Keep tucking – tight! smooth! – straight up the other side and you're home and dry. Now whip on that bedspread, making sure the overhang is equal on all sides and that there's enough at the head of the bed to cover the pillow plus a little extra. Why the extra? *So you can tuck it under the pillow edge* – you'll never need to be intimidated by this again.

Making the bed

The day-to-day act of bedmaking is relatively simple. First, make sure that the top and bottom sheet are still firmly tucked under the mattress – this is where fitted sheets are time-savers. Pull up the blanket, make sure it's straight and smooth, and fold the top few inches of the top sheet over the blanket. Then repeat the tucking routine and continue with bedspread and pillows as before.

No use taking the ostrich approach – leaving the top sheet and maybe even the blanket bunched up at the bottom of the bed and covering it up with the bedspread – out of sight, out of mind ... except that the sheet creates a nasty lump that's only magnified by the spread.

And don't let your sheets hang out – tuck those little devils in when they come loose. They look yukky peeking out from under the bedspread.

For those of you convinced it doesn't make any sense to make a bed "when you're just going to sleep in it again", there is a respectable way out. Minimize the number of blankets and covers you use – a couple of thick ones are better than four thin ones that you'll be half the morning smoothing and straightening out. Or buy a continental quilt that can serve as a bedspread too.

If you can dish it out, you can take it

Have you ever noticed the amazing sex change operation that occurs with the dishes? During the meal, they are the man's, but the minute all the food is slurped away, they become the woman's. Since the invention of the clay pot, men have schemed ways to escape doing the washing-up. They've sanded the wooden salad bowls, they've tried breaking things so they'd be thrown out of the kitchen, they've even stooped to claiming their hands are allergic to water (though it doesn't bother them to reach into a lake or river to unsnag a lure). All my life the girls or women

2. Never leave the plates. Scrape off the food: trying to wash plates plastered with potatoes and gravy, petrified pasta and hardened bacon is like having a bath with your clothes on.

3. Soak saucepans. Pots and pans and other heavy-duty utensils need to soak during the meal so the burned-on yuk in the bottom will soften for easier removal. And never *scour* that cast iron cookware unless you want to see how it looks with a coat of rust.

4. Dishwashers aren't robots or waste disposal units. Hard egg embedded on the cutlery will be there after the process – only more solidly. Scrape and rinse plates and dishes before putting them in the dishwasher. Unless you're dealing with lots of dishes, these automated units are slow and wasteful; you can get it done faster by hand. Likewise, waste disposal units aren't waste disposal units *unless you turn them on.* If you cram food down and don't flip the switch, all that awful stuff will stay there.

did the dishes and the men ... well, they disappeared.

I shouldn't have to use page space to tell you how to do the dishes, except that a few of you actually might not know how. I've been to your houses when your wife was out – you washed one plate at a time or were reduced to using the souvenir plates off the wall.

Don't be a dish dunce – go for it!

1. Carry dishes to the sink. Just taking your own (scraped) plate to the sink or kitchen worktop is a help. When ten people leave it to one person, it adds a lot of walking to the job of washing-up.

5. The hand washing process: Pile the cutlery into the water when you start and let it soak till the very end, to loosen encrusted food before washing. Glass, plastic and fragile objects

Well, gentlemen — shall we retire to the next room?

should be washed first while the washing water still has its full power – and before the heavy things are piled into a murky sink. Change the water whenever it goes grubby – which might mean three times, if the main course was spaghetti.

6. Use HOT water to wash and rinse with: the hotter the better, as hot as you can stand. The old argument of who washes and who dries is in fact obsolete – after you rinse dishes and plates under hot water, you don't have to dry them (unless we're talking about crystal goblets or other clear glass where a few water spots would be out of the question. Air dry-ing is surely more hygienic than rubbing them with a damp, dirty teatowel that's been hanging around the kitchen all week.

7. Surprise! Cleaning out the sink and sink outlet is part of doing the dishes.

8. As is wiping the table, and the kitchen cooking area. This has long been the secret knowledge of women, but wiping the worktops, top of the cooker, fridge door, etc., is part of the job and only takes seconds when the mess is fresh – leave them till later and you'll have to chisel them clean.

A man can (clean the bathroom)

All the girls at one secondary school leaped to their feet and gave me a surprise ovation for a single sentence I uttered in an assembly. All I asked the boys was, "Why do mothers, daughters and wives have to clean the outsides of toilets (and the floor around it) when men's inaccuracy caused the mess and smell?"

If the average man knew how much the average woman despises toilet splashes and shaving residue in, on and around the sink, soggy towels on the floor and scum in the bath and shower, he would clean up his act, and *fast.*

I give a professional course in the art of cleaning-a-bathroom-in-three-and-a-half-minutes on page 114 of *Is There Life After Housework?* which I highly recommend that you read. Lots of cleaning can be done by not dirtying the place in the first place; in ten minutes in the bathroom getting ready, we are creating thirty minutes of work. So in the bathroom, we should concentrate on three critical stages: before, during and after.

1. BEFORE ... We're quick to criticize a few extra cosmetic containers of hers, while our drawers and shelves have twenty bottles of after-shave (eighteen of which we never use), a rancid vial of Vitamin E, thirty-two disposable razors in various stages of disposability, the shaving brush and ordinary razor our mother-in-law gave us six Christmases ago, several half-empty cans of shaving cream, a mildewed loofah, wet match boxes, rusty tie-pins, prehistoric prescriptions, ruptured tubes of hair cream, combs with missing teeth, swollen trashy paperbacks, and a broken blow dryer. Don't worry about her things – clear yours up and there'll finally be room for the spare roll under the sink.

2. DURING ... While you use the bathroom you can:

Aim ... at the toilet and take care of "accidents" when they happen.

Take showers with the curtains inside the bath, so the floor and carpet don't get soaked.

Put that cap back on, brother! It takes exactly the same time to do it

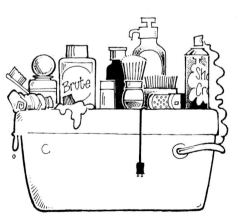

now as later – except by then it will have rolled down the drain or off down the hall.

Flossing teeth – although important – will never be an Olympic event. Lodged plaque freed by the floss sails out and sticks to the mirror. If you hold your head down when you floss or brush your teeth, any spatters will end up in the sink instead of on the mirror.

If you do get something on the mirror, give it a quick squirt with a spray bottle of glass cleaner, *not* a wet flannel, which will make it look twice as bad.

I nearly threw up – then I realised it was mine...

3. AFTER ... Put the toilet seat back down to save your beloved the chilling experience of cold porcelain on a bare bottom in the middle of the night.

Hair in the shower, bath or sink is just about the most revolting thing going. We leave it and it sticks to the side of the bath and outlet, sink top, etc. Sexy, isn't it? No way, sickening ... All we have to do is stand in the bath and drip dry while we slosh water around to flush the hair and gunk towards the outlet. Then pick it out. It's awful, but even worse if you have to do it for someone else.

Don't leave the wet bar of soap sitting on the edge of the bath, or the back of the toilet or sink. Put it in the soap dish.

Rinse away that stuff in the sink – whiskers, toothpaste, shaving cream, whatever. Any residue can be wiped away with a quick wipe of a nylon scrubbing sponge.

Wipe or squeegee down the walls after you shower.

Hang up your towel and flannel, and return your sailing boat to its slip.

Close all the drawers and put all the bottles and tubes back. (Metal cans will leave little rusty rings on porcelain if left on the sink).

Throw away those little scraps of tissue you've used to stop the flow of blood from shaving cuts.

And replace the toilet paper when it runs out instead of putting the new roll on top of the cistern for *her* to install.

Dust busting

Dusting is a relatively simple chore we tend to think of in "take it or leave it" terms. But it's not just dust, it's dead flies, orange pips, crumbs, wrappers, withered plant leaves and cobwebs that accumulate gradually on almost every household surface and can eventually erode even a castle. Dusting requires no vigorous training and any man, even the most busy, still has a few spare moments to pick up a duster and do this nagging little operation. Ten minutes of hustling will get the dusting done.

Dusting basics

1. You dust before you vacuum.

2. Dust from the top to the bottom.

3. A once-a-week once-over-lightly is enough for the average house.

4. Monthly, attack door frames, window blinds, curtains, light fixtures, skirting boards.

5. Dust lofts and rafters at least twice a year, using an extension handle.

Dusting is often most neglected and needed in high places that are hard for a woman to reach. Much of this is in stretch or reach territory – often guarded by a glaring spider or two. Even if you can't see the dust on the top of shelves or doors or on exposed supports or beams, it's there and getting rid of it in places like these will cut down on its circulation around the house. It will also discourage creepy crawlies from camping out and creating further mess.

You may be able to arrange a deal here: you do all the gruesome dusting (door frames, windowsills, unit tops, beams, fixtures, high furniture and curtain rails), while *she* does the tables, the plants, the knick-knacks and the details.

What do you dust with?

We men would never stoop to using an oily rag for dusting, and we wouldn't be caught dead with a feather duster. (Rags and feather dusters are not only ineffective, but actually worsen the problem). Dust control was my first lesson in large-scale commercial cleaning. We used a chemically treated paper dustcloth designed to pick up and hold dust and keep it out of circulation.

A good professional dusting tool is the Elbie Dustless duster, which is specially treated and collects dust without scattering it. It actually attracts dust with static electricity and is especially good for high places.

Put on the carpet

We men don't participate much in carpet care; we tread the dirt into it, lounge or wrestle on it, and maybe replace a threadbare piece once in a while – but that's about all. It's about time we were put on the carpet.

I'm not saying you should rush out and grab the vacuum cleaner from your wife. On the comment cards I've distributed to women in my audiences, I ask these two questions: "What is your favourite cleaning task? Your least favourite?" You may find this amazing, but *vacuuming* is overwhelmingly women's favourite. Is it the only chance they get to relax and dream ... or is it the soothing vibration ... or the "instant gratification" of vacuuming ... or maybe the sense of power? Who knows? But they love it, so let them keep it.

Vicarious vacuuming thrills

1. Keep the home supplied with a good machine. One out of every seven of you reading this needs a new vacuum cleaner *now*. They cost relatively little when you consider how much use they get, and how much pleasure a freshly vacuumed carpet can bring.

It's always worth paying for quality!

• Get a good upright model. You can buy an upright one for under £100 (see p.125). If you spend more than that, you're paying too much.

• Get a small wet/dry vacuum cleaner. These are available everywhere now for about seventy pounds.

2. Maintain your machines for top peak performance.

• Change or empty bags regularly – before the cleaner begins to lose pick-up power. This is the most important thing. People tend to put it off, but it's absolutely crucial to vacuum maintenance. Replaceable paper bags are preferable for home use, but if you have a cloth bag, shake it vigorously to get all the dust out of the fabric.

• Replace the belt every year or so; just have a look at it from time to time to see how it's wearing.

• Check the fan periodically to see if it needs to be replaced. The fans in some home vacuum cleaners are scarcely recognizable as such.

• Replace beater bars when worn; every two or three years get the motor cleaned.

• Don't confuse a vacuum cleaner with a compactor. These thingies weren't designed to pick up pennies, paper clips or vast quantities of cat litter. When string, thread or hair gets wrapped around the beater bar it will slow down the machine – turn off the cleaner immediately and remove anything that gets caught in there.

• And don't "borrow" the house vacuum cleaner to clean up the shed or cellar, or you may find yourself buying a new vacuum a lot sooner than you expected.

3. Clean up the trails. The traffic areas get dirty long before the rest of the carpet and need to be cleaned regularly to prevent unsightly paths from developing. (See How To Win at Housework, p. 62, and the revised edition of Is There Life After Housework?, p. 98).

Field guide to vacuum attachments

In the event you are called upon to wield the vacuum, here is a generic guide to attachments that will end, once and for all, that embarrassing quandary: "But which attachment do I use?" Attachments are available for canister, upright and wet-dry vacuums, but uprights tend to become awkward and tip over when you clamp on the converter needed to connect the attachments to the machine. Although they vary slightly from manufacturer to manufacturer, each species of attachment does have distinct characteristics that will aid you in identification.

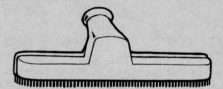

1. Crevice tool: A long, narrow tube with a flattened tip to reach into those hard-to-get-at places such as corners and the crevices at the sides of electric appliances.

3. Floor tool: A wide (approximately 12") head with brushes for vacuuming hard-surface floors; there is also a version without brushes for carpeting, called a rug tool.

2. Dusting brush: A small, usually circular brush for blinds, window-sills, skirting boards and shelves – anything that might get nicked if those little bristles weren't there to cushion things.

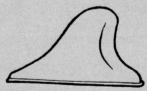

4. Upholstery tool: A small wedge-shaped nozzle – usually without brushes – used for cleaning upholstery, stairs and car interiors.

For canister vacuums only: Power head: a motorized head with beater brushes that really work that carpet over. If your vacuum has one, it will not only pick it all up – fast – but give you a sense of power and make the carpet looked "groomed" as well as litter-free.

For wet-drys: Squeegee head attachment for pushing water into a pool that can be vacuumed up much more easily.

4. Shampooing is really a man-size job (Hmm ... chauvinistic!) Yet we make our wives organise it whether we're doing it ourselves or hiring someone to do it. My expert opinion is that you pay a lot for shampooing in any case. Why not pay an expert and get it cleaned properly? Shampooing – if done correctly – actually extends the life of your carpet. Carpet cleaning is so competitive now, the prices are in the customer's favour. You can get it cleaned quicker, better and cheaper than you or your wife can do it. Even though I've been a professional carpet cleaner for thirty years, if I moved to a strange city and had a houseful of dirty carpets to deal with, I wouldn't hire the equipment and do it myself, I'd phone a local company.

5. Replace it. Carpet projects a psychological warmth; there is real emotion attached to its ownership, especially by the people who care for the home. The dirt, wear and damage to our carpet is absorbed into our feelings, so you really can relieve frigidity, fatigue and rebellion by doing a surprise good deed for the carpet. Next time you get the urge to buy a dressy coat, buy a furry floor covering instead. We men always ho-hum, stall and drag our feet to avoid a carpet confrontation, forcing the women to plead for a new or better one. No-body really wants the responsibility of choosing a new carpet, even though everyone immediately enjoys the benefits. So right now, put down this book, walk through the house, and when you spot your wife say something like, "Hey, you know the carpet in the living room has been down twenty-seven years and is looking really dreadful, looks like we need to do something about it, what do you think?" (You better try this in the vicinity of the couch, because when she faints on that thin, worn-out carpet it won't absorb much impact!)

If you only do these five things, you'll be worshipped and bragged about (and you're getting off lightly you old dog, you!).

Friendlier with the floor

A lot of years have gone by since most of you men reading this have been friendly to the floor: for most of us the floor is a vague uncharted region where crumbs fall and parts and coins roll away. Some of us must think we have the "self-cleaning" variety, the way we let ashes, crumbs and fingernail clippings fly.

Sweeping: You might think that good old standby, the broom, is hard to beat, but a small 12- or 18-inch commercial dust mop is far faster and more efficient on hard surface floorings like linoleum, vinyl, tile and wood. It catches that fine dust you can't get with a broom.

Mopping: That grease on top of your fridge is also on the kitchen floor; you just don't see it because it's been worked into the pattern. You have to wash a floor like anything else or it gets dirty, cloudy and sticky. (No matter what women claim, I know you wouldn't mop a floor without sweeping it first.)

Now here are some professional secrets for men only – you'll do it twice as fast as your woman and really surprise her. Use a neutral cleaner solution (see p.127) with a wet mop; water alone won't cut through it. Lightly wet the floor with the solution. Once doesn't do much – the first exposure to liquid acts as a wetting agent but it doesn't lift much grime. The wet shine says "clean" to your subconscious and you whip to the end brightening the floor a little but leaving a lot of residue. So wet the floor lightly, then dip the mop again in the cleaning solution. By the time you start again, the cleaner will have dissolved and suspended the grease, and it will be released from the floor surface. Mopping may cause a tiny bit of shine loss, but a day of use will polish off the few microns of detergent residue, so don't go piling on thirty new coats of polish.

How often should you mop a floor? It depends on the use it gets, but when your bare feet stick to the floor during your late-night snack, it's overdue.

Stripping a wooden floor: This is a repulsive job; any man who would make a woman do it shouldn't be able to sleep with a clear conscience. I can strip a floor faster than a team of twelve amateurs, and so can you. Once you master the pro way to go about this you'll be sought by all the neighbours, so keep it to yourself.

92

Stripping

This is to take off the old wax finish before applying the new.

1. Prepare a solution of commercial wax remover, following the directions.

2. Spread the solution on the floor in an area that you can handle at one time ... about 10' x 10' . Then leave it to dissolve the old hard wax and polish.

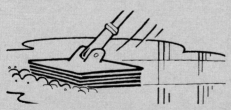

3. Now scrub with a scrubbing brush or floor machine with a stripping pad. Go over the area twice. (A scrape with the fingernail tells if the wax is dissolved.)

4. With an old squeegee or floor squeegee (not your window squeegee, see p.124), squeegee up the dirty, mucky slop water.

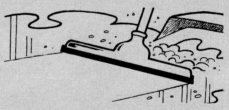

5. Then scoop the sloppy puddle into a dustpan and dispose of it.

6. Now rinse. Use a little vinegar in the rinse water to neutralize the floor. This is important because the stripper is highly alkaline and if the surface isn't neutralized the new wax won't bond to it.

Wish for wood

Whatever you do, don't let any woman cheat you out of caring for and cleaning the wood and wood panelling in your home. Caressing that luxurious grain is a really sensual experience. The fragrance of the oil soap you use for cleaning wood beats that of a Roman bath, and the whole process soothes and restores dignity to the soul. It's logical for us men to hog the job. We fell trees, we fashion it for domestic use, we might as well finish the job.

1. Don't believe the furniture polish propaganda. Ninety-five per cent of people use the stuff so thick on furniture and panelling that the insects could play on it and never slip off. Overpolished wood gets clogged up and looks hazy.

2. If you have raw or natural wood surfaces in your home, they'll need to be "fed" or treated to stop them drying out and cracking. Linseed oil and other such treatments should be rubbed on. Take your time so the wood can absorb it, then wipe off the excess.

I must admit I think feeding wood is a ridiculous waste of effort and material. If grease or ink get on bare wood, it's ruined. Low-gloss or satin-sheen finishes are available that seal the surface, forming a glass-like protective membrane through which that beautiful grain will still be bright and clear and fully visible. Marks and stains will end up on it instead of on the wood.

3. If you wish to apply (or reapply) a varnish or polyurethane membrane coat to ailing wood surfaces, it's easy. First, clean the surface with a strong cleaning solution – a strong ammonia solution, wax stripper or de-greaser if it's been sealed; solvent if raw – to take off all dirt and oils. Let it dry until any swollen grain goes down. Take care of any nicks or raised spots with a few strokes of superfine sandpaper, then wipe with a moist cloth or a cloth very lightly dampened with paint thinner to pick up any dust or lint on the surface. Finally, apply the varnish or polyurethane, paying attention to the directions on the container. It may need two coats.

Here's looking at you (through the window)

Have you noticed that even in your new Sebastian Coe designer running suit with matching Nikes people just don't notice you jogging down the street any more? Jogging lost its social edge some time ago and to go to all that effort without praise or pity, just for *exercise* alone is pretty grim. The everyday act of *window-cleaning,* believe it or not, is a hot new avenue for manly display and it's one hundred per cent productive as well as fun. It's been somewhat of a sleeper because it's been done with no class, with amateur tools like newspaper and vinegar. The female of the species has never really grasped the simple beauty of the job. All amateurs dread it, they fight it, they botch it. Go for it, boys! Window-cleaning is the most visible of all cleaning, inside or out, and it's fast and easy to do, the professional way. You are on the world's stage, you'll get all the glory! You've seen professionals turn out spotless shop windows and office blocks in seconds. You can learn to be just as good in minutes, I promise. Those handsome brass squeegees are inexpensive and last a lifetime. Here is all you do:

Six steps to sparkling windows

Go to a janitorial supplier and buy a professional-quality brass or stainless steel squeegee with a 10-, 12- or 14-inch blade.

Ettore Steccone brand is the only good squeegee available. Don't go to the local supermarket or superstore and buy those recycled lorry tyre war clubs they call squeegees. These won't work well even in a professional's hands. Make sure the rubber blade laps over both ends, and keep the blade undamaged – don't do anything but clean windows with it.

Pick up some window-cleaning solution, which can be either ammonia or ordinary washing-up liquid. Either will work well if you use them sparingly.

2. Wet the window lightly with the solution, using a clean sponge or brush. You don't need to flood it. You're cleaning it, not baptizing it! If the window is really dirty or has years of "miracle cleaner" gunk build-up, go over the moistened area again.

3. Wipe the dry rubber blade of your squeegee with a damp cloth or chamois. A dry blade on any dry glass surface will "peep-a-peep" along and skip places.

1. Put a capful of washing-up liquid in a bucket of warm water. There is always a tendency to add too much soap or detergent – this is what causes streaks and leaves residue.

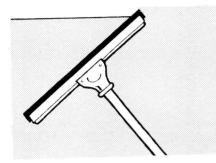

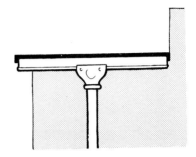

4. Next, tilt the squeegee at an angle to the glass so that only about an inch of the rubber blade presses lightly against the top of the window glass. Then pull the squeegee across the window horizontally.

This will leave about a 1-inch dry strip across the top of the window. Remember all those drips that came running down from the top of your clean window when you tried squeegeeing once before? Well, by squeegeeing across the top first, you've removed that potential stream.

6. ... and pull down, lapping over into the dry, clean area each time to prevent any water from running into the cleaned area. Wipe the blade with a damp cloth or chamois after each stroke. Finish with a horizontal stroke across the bottom to remove the water puddled there.

A window can be cleaned from either side or from the top using this technique. Always make sure you squeegee off that top inch of the glass first, to eliminate potential dripping. Wipe off the window sill with your damp cloth when you've finished. Exterior and interior windows are done the same.

Squeegees will work on any normal household window (not on textured or stained glass, for instance), and they can be cut to custom-fit your windows if you so desire.

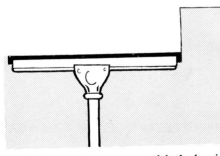

5. Place the squeegee blade horizontally in the dry area ...

What about drips, marks or lines?

Rags will smear or smudge.

Use your bare hand! The cleaning solution will have dissolved the oils in your skin and you can wipe off the small spots without leaving a mark.

As for the tiny $1/32''$ edge moisture, *leave it!* It will evaporate and won't be noticed.

Avoid the temptation to wipe it with a finger or cloth or you'll end up with a $1/2''$ streak.

Getting at high windows

When windows are out of reach for easy hand or ladder work, a pole or handle of any length you can manoeuvre will work on the same principle with surprising accuracy. I use a 4- to 8-foot extension handle.

Extension handle

Does second-storey windows quickly and your feet never leave the ground. No ladder is needed and there's no safety risk. (see p. 125).

Tap pole after each squeegee stroke.

Up against the walls

Cleaning walls and ceilings looms high on lists of housework, but it really isn't that much of a chore. If you make regular "spot cleaning" part of

98

your weekly household routine, they only need to be cleaned from top to bottom once or twice a year. Armed with a spray bottle of cleaning solution, you can keep even with the marks on every wall, door-frame, and light switch in your house in ten minutes on a Saturday morning.

When the time comes to *really* get the grime off all the walls and ceilings, remember that it's a lot harder for a woman to reach above her head because of the way her muscles are arranged. So tackle this job as a team: you take the ceiling and the upper half of the walls, and let her handle the walls lower down. With teamwork and the proper equipment, you can clean all the walls and ceilings in a big home in less than a day and actually enjoy doing it.

Washday wizardry

Gold, solid gold. They found it lying on the ground in the wild Alaska frontier; my daughter Karla, who lives in the wilds of Alaska, found a nice gold nugget, too, when she cleaned out a washing machine filter at the laundrette. Owning a classy laundrette in a town where 250 cruise shops dock yearly, she's made many amazing discoveries.

"Dad," she said "did you know that nine of ten men who come in here don't have a clue how to wash clothes."

"No!" I said incredulously.

"Do *you?*" (She dared to ask this of the world's Number 1 cleaning expert.)

My mind whipped back to the last time I tried to do the washing: when my wife Barbara was in hospital having our daughter Cindy (now twenty-one years old). "No, I don't," I admitted. "That washing machine's set of dials looks like the instrument panel of a 747."

I went home humbly and tried to do a load of washing. All nine of my best white shirts turned beige and I fried four Dacron shirts in the dryer. I know you're as tired of this ridiculous intimidation as I am, so I've consulted with expert females and reduced it all to the embarrassingly simple basics.

The ten commandments of washing

1. Sort clothes as follows: darks, delicate fabrics, whites, bright colours that don't run – bright colours that do or might run should be quarantined – and fuzzies (bathroom rugs and such, things capable of depositing fluff on everything in the machine). Make sure shirt sleeves aren't rolled up, socks aren't in a ball. Turn clothes right side out – except jeans, which will fade less if they're inside out. And don't wash things that shouldn't be machine washed. Silk and wool, for example, are usually hand washed or drycleaned. Check garment labels for instructions.

2. Pretreat stains. Alas, stains (grass, grease, tar, tomato sauce) will not necessarily be banished by the normal operations of washing and drying. Apply a pre-treatment product according to directions and the odds are much greater that you will be able to wear your trendiest sweatshirt to the company outing.

3. Don't overload the machine. There should be enough room in the tub for the clothes to *move freely* or they won't come out clean. When packed in too tight, they don't get clean, and this also puts extra strain on the machine. (Even it it does save a few bob at the laundrette!)

4. Use the correct programme setting. Many washing machines have instructions for use printed on the front. This will explain all the mysterious distinctions between gentle, rinse and spin, as well as critical basic information like how to turn the blasted thing on!

5. Use the correct water temperature. A reliable rule of thumb is hot

water for whites, warm water for medium and dark colours, cold water for bright colours and woollies. If your detergent doesn't work in cold water (check on the box), wash anything bright in warm water.

6. Don't use too much detergent. Check the box or bottle and *measure:* more is not better in this case. If you use too much detergent it won't rinse out, and the clothes will have a soap residue which can irritate skin.

101

7. Remove clothes promptly when the programme is finished. If you leave wet clothes in the machine for too long, the creases will set in and be twice as hard to iron out. Your mother was right, line drying is best for most fabrics, and the fresh air scent of wind-whipped sheets and clothes is better than any fabric softener. But many people use tumble dryers these days and only hang up the delicate clothes that shouldn't be tumble-dried. Check garment labels when in doubt about this.

8. Use the correct drying temperature. Some clothes should never be machine dried – your woollen jumper will fit a four-year-old just fine if you make the mistake of putting it in the dryer. Some garments should always be dried flat on a towel or other absorbent surface. (If you hang them up

Step one...
take off shirt...

to dry they'll stretch as well as develop unexpected epaulets on the shoulders.) Dryers are generally simpler to operate than washing machines.

Do make sure you clean the lint filter before using the dryer. Not only is that wad of lint clinging to the filter a fire hazard, it prevents the machine from operating at full capacity – the clothes may not get quite dry.

9. Remove clothes from the dryer promptly. Permanent press garments need to be removed while still slightly damp, or at the very least, hung up as soon as the dryer goes off. Otherwise, it's the creases that'll be permanent! Jeans and cotton·shirts will also be easier to iron if they're taken out when they're not quite dry.

10. Fold clothes and put them away. This too is part of the job. Keep a few hangers close to the dryer – if you hang clothes up while they're still hot from the dryer they'll be easier to iron.

More washday wisdom
● *If it's not dirty, don't wash it. The average family uses 2,000 towels in a year – that's a lot of washing hours. Used towels aren't dirty,*

Please – I'm down to my last shirt...

chairs, draped on doorknobs or stair railings, under the bed, under the covers in the bed, in the wardrobe or in your bottom drawer definitely doesn't count. By, on, or in the general vicinity of the basket won't score you any points, either.) Cleaning out the pockets will take on much more allure after the first time you wash your driving licence or your season ticket.

Are you a hot-shirt husband?

they're wet. A towel can go as long as a week. We can wear some working clothes several times, yet many people wash their work/garden clothes every day. On the other hand, if it's really dirty – muddy, greasy or gritty – wash it separately so the rest of the washing won't have to float in that grimy brine.

• If you need to use bleach it should be added at the beginning of the wash cycle when the machine is full of water, never full strength onto dry clothes, unless you want the splotched look beloved by teenagers.

• If you can't bring yourself to actually immerse yourself in the washing process, you can at least clean out your pockets before throwing your clothes in the laundry basket. (On the floor, over the backs of

Does your wife usually iron your shirt as you stand by the ironing board tapping your toes? I won't mention that you have fifteen shirts already pressed and hanging in the wardrobe, but just have to have your favourite one. A BBC presenter warmed up this subject by asking the studio audience, "How many of you men ironed the shirt you're wearing now?" Ten hands went up. "You're all single, aren't you?" They all were!

What is it, she asks, that happens to a man the minute he gets married that renders him incapable of ever ironing a shirt again? Do his ironing skills evaporate? No, they don't, but an iron will develops to never take care of his own washing and ironing.

A man's view of ironing is greatly altered by whether he is doing it or *she* is. If he's doing a shirt, front-and-collar alone is good enough any day; if she is, the whole thing needs to be done – and well. In this day of fuss free fabrics and cheap and convenient professional services, ironing shirts is slave labour. Buy clothes that don't need it, and if you're insane enough to insist on 100 per cent cotton, send them *out* to be ironed.

Strike while the iron is hot.

1. Turn the iron on to the proper heat setting. Do read that little label on the garment, or you'll read it later and weep. You'll be glad to know that the iron itself – the print on the temperature selection – will help you out here.

● Don't be unduly impressed by the labels "drip-dry" and "permanent press". You will probably, in the famous housecleaner's term, have to "touch these up" a bit with the iron at a low setting, unless you're into the rumpled look.

● Don't use too hot an iron on synthetics or "delicate fabrics" unless you're looking for an excuse to never wear it again.

2. Place the article to be ironed on the ironing board (or pillowcase or towel if there's no ironing board in sight). Corduroy and wool are ironed inside out – unless you want crushed corduroy and shiny suits.

3. The mystic act of dampening might be desirable if the item is severely wrinkled or made of cotton or linen. Dampening simply means sprinkling with water – which can be done with a few fast flicks of a wet hand, if necessary.

● Steam, if you can face this subtlety of the process, is almost as good as sprinkling – and actually better on some things for banishing wrinkles. You do have to put water – preferably distilled – into the iron, to get steam.

4. A standard man's shirt should be ironed in the following order:

● Collar – back of collar first, then front.
● Shoulder area or "yoke".
● Cuffs – inside first, then outside, then sleeves.
● Front pieces – it's best to iron the button strip or "placket" on the reverse side first.
● Back or body.
● If you're of the stiff-collar school, use a squirt of spray starch as you iron each piece.

5. Place the shirt on a hanger,

fasten the top button and hang it in the wardrobe.

And we shall be rewarded a hundred-fold ...

It's men who really have the reputation for snappy folding – those faultlessly folded regimental flags, intricate paper aeroplanes and the perfect creases in our trousers. And who can correctly refold a road map as well as a man? We once had the ability to perfectly fold tents, sails and tarpaulins, but somehow we've evolved to stuffing, draping and throwing things. A ten pound note is about the only thing most of us males fold any more. Some of us might fold the clothes in our suitcase if a woman isn't there to do it for us, and of course we can fold our arms when housework hovers ...

Folding is a good way to ease into housework because it can be done while doing something else, such as watching TV or swapping stories. Here are a few assignments to get us back in practice.

Towels and flannels. It's time to quash that ugly rumour that we can't fold anything we take out of the dryer. Even fitted sheets and king-size bedspreads are not nearly as difficult as you might imagine. If

See? Perfectly folded!

you fold towels lengthwise first, you won't have to refold them before hanging them on the towel rail.

T-shirts, shorts, pyjamas – any clothes put back on a shelf or into a drawer.

The Sunday paper, if you're the first one to read it.

Socks deserve a special mention. More than a few of us have stooped to buying new socks rather than face pairing up the old ones. Though not exactly folding, the pairing of socks is similar and not an operation beyond technological comprehension. Even *women* have managed to reduce this to a few simple clues of colour, length, base material and pattern!

Who's got the button?

I resent the accusation that we men never sew on buttons. It has nothing to do with willingness or skill – the problem is *availability*. (Notice, we always keep the loose button.) Women keep that fantastic collection of buttons, needles and thread actually hidden from us. Give us access to those sewing items and we men will show you some precision buttonhood. Of course, a few of us may need a little refresher in the basic operations involved here.

Once you've laid your hands on that sewing basket, assemble your materials, button(s), item to be buttoned, needle, thread and scissors.

Material check:

Needle. Bigger is better, but a darning needle is usually too big. I use as large a needle as will fit through the buttonhole.

Thread. If you're sewing a button that only has an eye on the back, you don't have to worry about the colour because the thread won't show. Otherwise, match your thread to that of the surviving buttons.

If you can't find the exact colour, use a slightly lighter shade. If you're sewing on a coat or jacket button, use heavy-duty thread.

Operations:

Thread the needle. Moisten the end of the thread before attempting to insert it through the needle's eye. (Now you see why I like big needles.)

Pull the thread through the eye till the ends are even and knot the ends together so you have a double strand.

Sew the button back on. Place the button in the proper position to be sewn.

Start on the underside of the garment and poke the needle up through a button eye; pull the thread up through. Then poke the needle down through another eye and pull through and so on. If it's a four-eye button, see how the other buttons are stitched (criss-crossed, side to side?) and do yours the same way.

Stitch the button at least five times; generally, the more stitches the less likely that you'll have to repeat the button-sewing procedure again soon.

If it's a button that gets a lot of tugging, leave a little slack between the button and fabric surface each time you pull through. This will raise the button up a little and make it easier to use, especially on thick, bulky garments. Even a lot of women don't know that trick!

After you've made your five stitch-throughs, wrap your thread around the "stalk" or shank several times. Leaving the slack you need for a shank can be accomplished more easily by slipping a matchstick over the top of the button before you start. Then when you've finished stitching, pull the matchstick out and you're ready to start wrapping the thread around the shank. Secure your handiwork on the backside by making a few last stitches and knotting the thread back on itself. *Mission accomplished.*

Finish the job. Snip the thread as close to the knot as possible and return those sewing supplies to the basket, *now,* before you forget, or you may not get the applause you deserve for finally getting a grip on your own lost buttons.

Begin the "behind"

In thirty years as a husband and home-owner, despite the fact that I was a professional cleaner, I never *once* moved anything to get behind it. Why was that? Because a little voice inside me always whispered, "That's the usual cleaner's job." All the rest of you men have heard and obeyed the same little voice. Even when we don't mind cleaning and gladly jump in, we never move or get behind or under anything, or in the back of it, because we feel we are just helping out with the duties of the usual cleaner (the woman).

This of course is not our fault; it's a woman's – our mother's – who after cleaning our messy little behind, wrestled us down and cleaned behind our ears, and she cleaned under our bed, too. We grew up accustomed to not being responsible for what we couldn't see (though in our youth we might have got behind the cushions a couple of times to retrieve any change that might have rolled out of Dad's pockets). In the thousands of housecleaning questions I've been asked by men and women over the years, I've never, ever had a man ask about anything that has to do with behind or under doors or appliances or furniture. I've worked out why, too. We men are natural exhibitionists. There is no credit or glory behind closed doors; men don't fight in private behind the pub, they do it in the street and often wait for the TV camera and press to get there before starting. The only behind that gets unsolicited attention from us is the female variety.

Ring the police! It's Lord Lucan!

Well, men, we need to make up for being surface polishers and centre-line cleaners and jump into the realm of "down under" cleaning. The fact is, women really hate to get behind and under. They've done it all their lives, but it's hard on them. Getting in behind and under things always means ugly bugs and mice and spiders scurrying out. There are dead and rotten things behind and under and in the back of, and the simple strain and weight of moving appliances and furniture to get at unseen areas really is, if we can excuse an outdated phrase, a job for a man. Trying to move something too heavy always results in injuries to the floors, walls and the unit, as well as often to the person doing the trying.

This is a task that only has to be done a couple of times a year; it should be a walkover for us. So one Saturday morning, casually tell her that you're taking on the duties of the hard-to-get-to, seldom-seen and often-forgotton places – and then get on with it. Here is a map of behinds that will yield a treasure of appreciation (not to mention two or three of the things you've been looking for all year).

Remember: If you get behind any large appliance make sure you unplug it or are careful of the gas pipe. You'll live to enjoy the results – she still likes you better than the insurance money.

Cooker: Pull the cooker away from the wall; pad the feet of appliances with an old towel so they are easier to pull-out. The floor back there may be really gungy, so be prepared to let your cleaning solution soak for a while. Once the floor is clean, use a vacuum cleaner to pick up any dust in the corners, and slide the appliance back.

Refrigerator: Refrigerator experts tell me the dust and grease that collect in the coils and fan area of a refrigerator cause the majority of the repair problems as well as reduce the life of the unit. Unplug the refrigerator, pull it out and vacuum the "fluff" (dust) off the coils. You can also use a carpet brush or a handle with a damp cloth wrapped around it. Wipe up the debris on the floor, then slide the unit back.

Washing machine and dryer: All these machines will find a way to gather a junk cache – lint, fluff, odd objects that fell off the washer (out of the pockets you forgot to empty), things roaming or being swept across the floor, spilled soap powder, odd socks, all of this will collect behind them.

Pull out the appliance, sweep up the clutter, then wash the back of the washer or dryer with disinfectant cleaner.

Couch and chairs: These might seem simple, but they can be a real drag if you try to *drag* them on the carpet. So lift them out (with two or three small moves, not one giant heave), vacuum and de-clutter behind and replace.

Bed: A certified doctor of dust said the average home accumulates forty pounds of dust annually. I'm convinced most of it ends up under the bed, where it can settle and lie undisturbed for long periods of time. Vacuum cleaners can be hard to manoeuvre under here, so try a slightly damp dust mop – it works superbly on carpeting. Or move the bed over and then vacuum underneath.

Pictures: Ah yes, we dust the fronts but that's about it. Once a year or so, take them down, dust the frame and back, and rehang (we men ought to have a better eye for getting them straight, anyway).

To do all of the behind work in the whole house will take you a few hours at most. An easy trade-off for five or six hours of other tedious chores. You can knock this off on Saturday morning and have a clear conscience through the whole Saturday afternoon sports programmes.

Compliance with appliances

Most of us are impressed that ships are officially female but more impressive, if you think about it, is the sex slant of appliances. Men benefit fifty per cent (or more) from appliances, yet they are all "hers": *her* washing machine, her cooker, her mixer, her vacuum cleaner. (Did you ever hear a man call out, "Where's our vacuum cleaner, dear?" It's all "hers", right down to "her" can opener. Even the kitchen is "her" kitchen and the sink "her" sink.

Ownership is probably psychologically absorbed from custodianship. Since we don't often clean them, we can ignore them until they break down. But between their first step and their last stumble there is a thing called *"upkeep"*, which is a manly calling. Upkeep involves cleaning up such things as dried milk down the inaccessible back or side of an appliance, dust accumulation in grills and motors, and burned, caked-on grease in the burner area. One evening or early Saturday morning, it would be downright macho to start a relationship, a kind of vicarious infidelity, with

these "she" appliances – service and clean them.

Spend more time soaking and less time scrubbing!

To clean the exterior of any major appliance – cooker, refrigerator, washing machine or dryer – follow these easy steps.

1. Using a spray bottle, squirt on a solution of heavy-duty cleaner or grease cutter. A high butyl content cleaner (like wax remover) really works on the grease ... *fast!!!*

2. If you need to scrub, use a soft nylon pad, *don't* use scouring powder, steel wool, rugged nylon pads or metal scrapers. You'll scratch the finish.

3. Let the cleaning solution remain on the surface for a while to soften and dissolve the dirt and grease.

4. Then wipe it off with a soft towel or cloth. If you want the unit to really shine, spray it with glass cleaner and wipe again.

Cookers

require some special treatment in addition to the above, because grease droplets and burned-on stains are really tough to remove.

1. Start by taking the burners out, if possible, and soaking them in hot, soapy water while you're cleaning the top.

2. Your nylon pad or sponge will take care of the softer baked-on grease, but you may need to resort to a scouring pad to get rid of those encrusted grease droplets. (The sharp edges of the pad will pick up the bumps, and if you keep it wet it won't hurt the surface.) Rinse the pad occasionally with hot water to remove the accumulated grease.

3. Then rinse the burners and replace them. (They may still need a little scrubbing.)

4. Wipe the cooker top, front and sides with glass cleaner, and your cooker will sparkle like new.

Conquering the caves

Houses are full of hidden places that provide an invisible serving of housework. We men constantly pass by the outside, almost never experiencing beyond. *Someone has to go in there* – why not us for a change? What gentleman would send his lady down in the mine, through a dangerous tunnel, into a chasm of beetles and bats? Here are some house caves to explore and de-chore:

Fridge and freezer

A man is about as likely to enter these enclosures to "clean them out" as he is to intentionally walk into a women's toilet. Refrigerators are the acknowledged domain of the female (though we may actually use the fridge more).

Should you be able and willing to face "the big clean-out" – it doesn't take a strong stomach and nerves of steel – here is the procedure.

1. Take everything out of the refrigerator.

2. Mix a solution of 1½ oz. ammonia or disinfectant cleaner in three gallons of water.

3. Wash all surfaces with a soft nylon sponge; wet down and sponge off hardened food.

4. If possible, remove the wire shelves, the vegetable drawers and the cooler tray and wash these in the sink.

5. Then dry and buff all areas with a soft, clean cloth, and replace contents of refrigerator.

The unspeakable oven

First of all, don't believe *anything* comes off "easily". No matter what you use, including "miracle overnight soaker", this is going to be hard, dirty work. As professional cleaners using the same types of chemical oven cleaners you do, the only magic we've found is patience. Cover those sticky blobs with cleaner and don't be over-anxious to start wiping off. Make sure there's plenty of ventilation; let the solution work even longer than it says on the label. It will almost certainly save scraping and grinding. I like nylon scrubbing pads (such as Scotch-brite); they get into the revolting spots around the elements, corners and cracks. *Here's the secret women never knew* – when it all doesn't come off, it means the solution ran out of oomph before it dissolved all the grease. So instead of violently scrubbing the remaining spots, just apply a second coat of solution and you can wipe it off in seconds (after you *wait*).

The cooking vents and grilles

Cooking grease, dust, etc., are constantly sucked into kitchen vents. A vent can get half an inch thick with grease and become smelly, as well as a real fire hazard. I've cleaned thousands of vents professionally – it only takes a few minutes and you can and should (about once a year) take care of this ceiling cave.

First unscrew the cover plate or grille. Put it in a sink full of hot water and strong grease cutter such as ammonia or wax stripper along with any filters there may be. Let them soak while you work on the rest of the unit. Next reach up into the flue opening and unplug the unit – the motor and fan should slip out easily. Clean off the grease with paper towels and a spray bottle of degreaser solution, being careful not to make anything electrical wet or spray anything into the motor. Now spray off the grille and filters with steaming hot water. Dry everything thoroughly and reassemble. Replace the charcoal filter in non-vented units as necessary.

Rubbish removal

Just over the page there is an Official Rubbish Remover's Appraisal Form, so you can assess your performance in this most manly of male jobs. For years we could get an A grade in housework by performing the simple act of taking out the dustbin. (Even so, we didn't necessarily do it, of course). Our new household consciousness obviously calls for some revised standards here.

OFFICIAL RUBBISH APPRAISAL

Aspects of Performance	Far Exceeds Job Requirements	Exceeds Job Requirements
TIMELINESS	Takes out the rubbish before the first Kleenex hits the bottom of the bag	Takes out the rubbish the minute there are smelly paint rags or a rotten fish
INITIATIVE	Looks for opportunities to take out the rubbish	Takes out rubbish without being asked
THOROUGH-NESS	Scrubs and disinfects rubbish bins every week	Puts in a new liner every time he empties the bin
FORM	Sorts refuse into recyclables and rubbish	Picks up his failed basket rim shots and pops them in the basket
AESTHETICS	Allows no smell of rubbish in the house	Buys good rubbish liners to keep odour down
ATTITUDE	Buys shares in a refuse company	"It is my job to handle the rubbish"

REMOVER'S FORM

Meets Job Requirements	Needs Some Improvement	Does Not Meet Minimum Requirements
Takes out the rubbish when the kitchen bins or waste-paper baskets are full	Takes out the rubbish when it overflows	Takes out the rubbish when it overflows all over the house
Takes out the rubbish when asked	Takes out the rubbish when threatened	"Take out the rubbish? What rubbish?"
Takes dustbins to pavement every week and brings back	Takes dustbins to pavement every week	Couldn't tell you what day dustmen come
Drops things on the way to the bin, but picks them up	Drops things on the way to bin and leaves them there	Can't even find the dustbin or wastepaper basket
Rubbish smells inspire him to take out the rubbish	Rubbish smells intrigue him	Rubbish smells resemble him
"I will help with the rubbish"	"Only when it's my turn"	"I wouldn't touch the rubbish"

Chapter Seven

It's only natural for men to find a better way

The importance of good tools and equipment

A gross injustice is usually inflicted on the housecleaner in this area. Over and again, in home after home, I see a rickety old vacuum cleaner, hardly capable of running, let alone sucking up any dirt. Every day people wrestle with these machines doing the housework, while in the basement or garage sits an expensive chain saw or other power tool that hasn't been used in six months. These tools give our masculinity an occasional boost – while others fight with an unsafe, ineffective vacuum cleaner for hours every week. Take a look at your kingdom of things and you may find it a little embarrassing that you have routers, special spanners, wrenches, electric rotivators, etc., that save a little time once or twice a year, while in the kitchen or laundry area your family struggles on, day after day, with antiquated tools and equipment.

In most cases, after an industrious project or two, we seldom use the expensive gadgets and tools we bought for our hobby; as investments go, such tools are poor ones. *Our time is our most valuable commodity,* and good housecleaning tools and equipment can save hundreds of hours a year.

For a modest investment, for example, you can buy a top vacuum *and* a wet-dry vacuum cleaner for your home, making it easy and inviting for all the family to hoover up. Husbands and wives should take a serious look around their houses. Some ironing boards could go in a museum – yet a safe new one costs only a few pounds! Think of a modern washing machine, a tumble dryer, a trouser press or some nonstick pots and pans. The tools likely to be used most and those capable of saving the most time are the ones that should be purchased. Avoid fancy attachments to cleaning machines or appliances of any kind. Stick to solid basic tools and supplies.

And Ah, the economy of it all

There are more benefits from using the right equipment and supplies than merely doing a faster and better job.

There is *safety:* you will be using fewer, simpler items that will be safer to use and store.

Cost: you will spend seventy-five per cent less on cleaning supplies if you select and use them properly.

Depreciation: using proper cleaning supplies and tools reduces damage to and deterioration of the surfaces and structures you're cleaning.

Storage: few flats, mobile homes, or, for that matter, houses have enough storage space, and the right items will take up much less space than the arsenal of cleaning preparations you're using now.

There ae some good inexpensive tools that should be in every home to make cleaning easier. They should be carefully chosen – *to-*

gether! Now, don't go buying these for Mother's Day or birthdays; this isn't *her* gift, it's for the *family* ...

And don't forget to think professional. All the best equipment is at the janitorial suppliers, not the cheapy department stores where most women have to shop. You – yes you, Mr Ordinary Citizen – can buy professional cleaning supplies and equipment.

What can a man do? Replace it!

We easily accept the fact that brakes, tyres, clothes and footwear have a natural lifespan and have to eventually be replaced, but household things we somehow envisage lasting forever. *They don't.* Homemakers by the millions are battling with worn-out baths, damaged drawers, clapped out ironing boards and cupboard doors that won't stay shut. Because curtains just hang there, we think they should last forever.

Not so. Even "indestructible" concrete paths crack, flake and deteriorate and not only look bad but require twice the time and expense to keep up. Toilets wear out, light fixtures often have a short life. Washing machines may function but the new models may do twice the work. If we men did nothing

but keep the household equipment and structures fully functional, that alone would be an untold aid to housework.

A good example is the cooker top. In thousands of homes I've seen tops with a stained and chipped surface, non-working dials, rickety knobs that are cracked or lost and grills blackened beyond belief. Yet because at least three of the burners will heat (with a little coaxing and some clever juggling), it stays. A new, safe, and much more attractive model only costs £150-£200!

I've cracked it!
I've bought the house next door!

Be a man – replace it with something new, better, easier to clean

Little or no expertise is needed, and often very little cash! Do-it-yourself stores are dripping with new, smarter, safer and stronger fixtures! New is easier, emotionally and physically, to care for.

Improved storage – better than a room full of roses

You can design or build things to make the house easier to clean and live in, or just to make more room. If you've been trying to come up with the ultimate gift or act to impress your companion, if dinners and flowers have been falling flat,

lead her blindfolded into a giant new "just for her" storage area. Pull off the blindfold, and the scream of delight will be unequalled. We men make fun of the female's crammed storage area, when the truth is we men have the majority of cubic feet. A friend was ranting that his wife filled every crack with sewing, recipes, souvenirs ... in the next breath he said all I have is the garden shed and the garage (790 cubic feet – his wife had four cupboards and the space under the stairs – 91 cubic feet). And when the children come home for a visit, or leave a few things till they see how the move or the new job works out, etc., in whose space do they pile their stuff?

Don't try to find more storage space in the existing structures; women can do that by instinct. *Make* more storage space.

1. Convert no-longer-used rooms into live storage space.

2. Shelves mounted on walls can create a lot of new space in places where you need it most.

3. Build or install cupboards or shelves in those cluttered but condensed areas like the cellar, attic and garage.

4. Move seldom-used, seasonal or never-used stuff to the loft (better still, throw it out).

5. Yes, consider a little shed in the back garden.

If the worst comes to the worst, sacrifice some of yours. Lack of good convenient storage space is the single biggest complaint I get from women at my seminars.

You can design or build housework out

Use "maintenance-free" materials when you remodel or build. These are often the opposite of what we expect. A few examples:

Glass: is great. You don't have to texture it, sand it or paint it. Children won't write on it, you don't have to hang pictures on it, it doesn't depreciate, and no matter how dirty it gets, it's "psychologically clean". The only thing glass needs is to be cleaned once or twice a year and we men can do that with a squeegee in a minute.

Masonry: Beauty is in the promise of function, and from that point of view masonry may just be the most beautiful material. It insulates well, it can't be destroyed, it won't burn or rot. Its strength gives a sense of security as it resists all manner of physical abuse. People even tolerate soiled concrete because it serves unyieldingly – dirt blends in with the surface and a few cobwebs give it class.

Laminate: We should all give our homes a little "plastic surgery".

Plastic laminate!

Today's laminates can look so much like wood, iron or fabric that they fool even mother nature. Plastic surfaces resist just about all stains and dirt, and we can find a shiny or textured plastic finish to match our every aesthetic want and whim. Laminate resists damage, kids' cars, sun, food and pet attacks. It's a true maintenance-free material, and here to stay.

Bear in mind, when you're designing or remodelling, that the more different kinds of materials and surfaces you have in a room, the more equipment and *time* it will take to clean it.

TICK! ... Before you begin to clean.

Some things can't be cleaned. Others will look tatty even when they're clean and orderly. Taking care of these things first will make cleaning and maintenance a lot easier. It'll also get these nagging little items off your "to do" list once and for all.

Eliminate or remove anything that bugs you, that's inconvenient, no longer functional, or you just don't like. *Remember* – the first principle of efficient cleaning is not having to clean in the first place.

Fix the things that slow you down and cause wasted effort.

Make sure there are plenty of waste paper baskets and rubbish bins. ☐

Light bulbs are replaced as needed. ☐

That every leaky or dripping tap is repaired. ☐

Label all fuse boxes. ☐

Drawer hardware is tight and drawers slide easily. ☐

Paint all surfaces that are hard to dust, wash or clean. ☐

All dirt and air leakage into the house is stopped. ☐

All windows slide open and shut easily (and lock) and cracks are closed. ☐

All concrete floors and unfinished wood surfaces are sealed for easy maintenance. ☐

Get rid of any furniture you aren't using or don't need. ☐

Make tops of all doors smooth and dustable. Light sanding and two coats of varnish or lacquer will do the trick. ☐

Get rid of or pad all head and shin bumpers. ☐

Stair banisters, clotheslines, etc., are all tightened. ☐

Old rough walls, battered skirting boards, chipped paint, cracked windows and leaky taps all make work. Most of us don't mind wiping a fingerprint or a black mark off the wall if a flick of the cloth will do it, but if it's a roughly textured or cheaply painted surface, cleaning will be put off indefinitely.

Faulty household furnishings and fittings can inflict an instant pre-defeat on those who clean them. The fact that most men haven't done much cleaning is the easy explanation for why these things are still being cajoled and cuddled along. It's the woman who's always trying to squeeze another ounce, inch or hour of life out of them (while we men are out playing squash or watching football with our friends). It amazed me how quickly I found inexpensive replacements when I finally had to sweep, scrub or clean a long-gone gadget.

Professional equipment

Spray bottles: For most general and regular cleaning, you'll want pint or quart plastic trigger-spray bottles to fill with the cleaning solutions you mix from concentrated cleaners, disinfectant, ammonia or washing up liquid.

Wet/dry vacuum: Used for all household vacuuming; to pick up water when scrubbing floor, to pick up spills and overflows. Make sure you get one with a rust-resistant tank and attachments.

& supplies

Professional window kit: lifetime brass Steccone squeegee, extension handle and applicator wand are exactly the same as the pros use. You can become an expert in minutes. The whole set costs only £18.

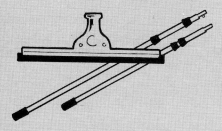

Heavy-duty floor squeegee: Does a super-smooth job that beats mops on wet surfaces. Cuts floor/pathway water removal/pick-up time dramatically.

Upright commercial vacuum: The big hotel contractors who clean hundreds of thousands of square feet of carpet daily use a light (20-pound) commercial model. These powerful machines are more effective and more economical than home models.

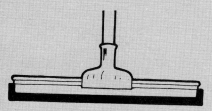

Good old wooden or metal-handled stiff garden broom: The fast way to sweep concrete floors and paths – no more supermarket saggers!

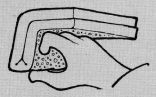

Dry sponge: (my favourite cleaning tool.) Cleans flat-painted walls and ceilings, wallpaper, lampshades and oil paintings like magic. Cleans many surfaces better, faster and less messily than liquid cleaners.

Hand floor scrubber: A £14 tool – a nylon pad on a handle – that will outwork a 150-horsepower floor machine. Does corners, edges, skirting boards easily – you'll never have to go on hands and knees again.

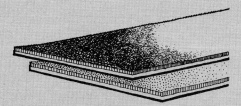

Commercial mats: Nylon or olefin fibre with vinyl or rubber backing. The exact same ones that are used in banks, schools and department stores. These should be placed for at least two steps both inside and outside every external door. They're safe – won't slip – and last for years. Save hundreds of hours of housecleaning by preventing tracking in of dust, grit and other debris.

Dust mop: The fast and efficient way to clean hard floors. Treat occasionally with dust-mop treatment for best results. Shake out or vacuum head regularly; wash when dirt-saturated, then re-treat.

Concentrated commercial cleaners: Three basic types (which you can buy for bout £4) – heavy-duty neutral cleaner, disinfectant cleaner, and alcohol-based glass cleaner – will do almost every cleaning job you need done in a house and will replace £50 worth of cupboard-cluttering cans, jars, sprays, tins and bottles.

Phosphoric acid cleaner: Removes hard water and mineral deposits, body oil and soap build-up from tiles and fixtures – pleasant, safe and powerful!

WARNING: Some of these concentrated cleaning chemicals can be dangerous. Don't forget to store them where they can't be reached by children.

Finding supplies

Because these items have been tested by the 2,000 or so professional cleaning people in my company they are not the usual – often junky – gadgets found in High Street shops. You will need to look for janitorial suppliers in the yellow pages and go where the professionals shop.

You will also be helped by Jaymart (Tel: Westbury (0373) 864926) who supply the correct matting. Diswinco Supplies Ltd. (1, Southsea Road, Kingston-on-Thames, Surrey KT1 2EJ, Tel: 01-546 1140/1191) supply almost all the products on this list, including the dry sponges. Batley & Co. (Tel: 061-480 3880) supply the Elbie Dustless Dusters, described on page 88.

A more complete list and description can be found on pp. 21 to 24 in Is There Life After Housework?

Chapter Eight

Professional help: give it or get it

Professional help: give it or get it

Cleaning and cooking are the big ones that can send any woman packing, especially if she's trying to cope with the other demands of a family and/or an outside job. We all know that the recent explosion of convenience foods has taken some pressure off the feeding end, but few of us know that outside cleaners can also provide a giant home relief valve. There are cleaners and companies that can clean your house faster, better and cheaper than you could yourself. Sometimes calling in the professionals makes the same wonderful time-saving sense as getting rid of an old twin-tub washer and investing in an automatic model. In the busy world of jobs, career and children, some outside help can be a saviour, and it's not out of reach of the ordinary man. You think she'll be insulted? *No way!* What do you think she'd take if you gave her a choice between a once-a-week dinner on Saturday night at £30 or a once-a-week cleaner for £15 and the extra £15 in her pocket?

When to call for help

In everybody's life, there's a time to call for help. I'd call when:

1. There are time limitations – the housework is becoming overwhelming because of all the other things you and your spouse *have* to do.

2. There are physical limitations – your place is just too big for the pair of you to handle, or one or both of you is in some way restricted in the kinds of physical tasks you can undertake.

3. It's the financially correct decision if your wife is offered a top job

– but only if she works full time. (Would *you* take a low paid part time job so you could fit in more housework!)

4. A job is too high, too big, too special or you just don't have the knowledge to do it.

5. Renting or finding the equipment will cost more than hiring someone to do it.

6. You just want to give a thoughtful, heartwarming gift ... wow!

What kind of professional help?

As housework is often more than whisking up a bit of dust and adjusting an off-centre lamp, so is there a difference in the types of professional people you can hire to come and do "your housework". Many cleaners and cleaning services are essentially a sort of skim service. They often won't do any of the real housework like cleaning outside windows, ovens, washing carpets or stripping and waxing floors. They may do these "big jobs" for a special hourly rate, but usually they just scoot in and dust, vacuum, straighten, tidy – and go.

Cleaners charge by the hour (usually in the range of £2.00 to £3.00 an hour) or by the visit. Should you use a cleaning company or an independent? Independent cleaners have both more to gain and more to lose by pleasing you – or not pleasing you. Think about what the services offered will be worth to you,

not only in terms of cost but in terms of time freed for other things. The cost to you will depend on how many times a week or a month your house needs attention to prevent minor chores from piling up. You may even decide that since you (or your kids) can do the same work just as fast for nothing, you'd rather spend the time than the money after all. By doing it yourself you'll eliminate lots of arranging and key-handling and interruptions to home life. There's no home cleaning job a man can't do well ... if he wants to!

Employ a cleaner on a trial basis to begin with. You might get someone useless the first couple of times, but keep advertising and in a month or so you'll find someone reliable who works at a reasonable rate. When you find somebody good, talk to them about returning weekly, monthly or whatever. You need help you can count on, and if those you hire know they'll be getting regular work, they're more likely to accept the going rate.

A professional cleaner (as opposed to a domestic help) is the heavy-duty type. These people do more than briskly brandish aerosol and pine scent, they do the big heavy jobs calling for big heavy equipment. Call professional cleaners when you have a big, one-time or seasonal job.

Who to call in

There are many cleaning companies in the Yellow Pages, in newspapers, in classified ads, and in local shop window ads everywhere. Cleaning services have multiplied dramatically in the last ten years. But a word of warning is called for here – some of these "professionals" are experimenting amateurs and some (more than we fellow professionals would like to admit) are destruction on wheels and casters.

Don't fall for inflated claims, including the classics: "We're big enough to do anything and small enough to care", etc. Remember, reputation is the most important criterion for selection – and for your protection. When you're shopping for a service, whether long or short term:

1. Ask them how many years they've been in business. This isn't a foolproof indicator, but it helps. In this business, there's a very high failure rate, and the people who make it and stick with it for five years are generally reliable and competent.

2. Get three to five references and phone them. This *is* worth your time, because you may be selecting someone who'll be doing your work for years to come, or you may be

131

risking a £500 couch or chair – if they ruin it, it's your problem. Remember, workmanship isn't insurable: you'd have to sue.

3. Ask who will actually *do* the work – will it be the person whose name is on the business card, the wonderful friendly voice on the phone or will the job get farmed out to a couple of layabouts who'll be causing havoc and kicking your cat around? Know what you're getting into, to eliminate unpleasant surprises later.

Get an estimate

For big, one-off jobs, get an estimate. I'd never have a cleaning crew working for me by the hour. With an estimate, both parties know well in advance what they're in for. Estimates are usually quotes in terms of square feet (to be cleaned, shampooed, stripped, whatever). Have a complete list of what you want done ready. Ask them to outline exactly what they'll do, for how much. If they're competent and professional, they'll know how long each part of the job will take and how much it'll all cost. If they can't or won't give a firm estimate, I personally would phone somebody else. Getting an estimate is very simple, but *most important*.

And when you get their estimate (written and *signed*), make sure you check their insurance coverage. Do they have *public and product liability insurance* (in case there's an accident, they burn the house down, break the front window or have a fight and kill each other)? Remember, it's all going on in your house and *you* are responsible if they don't have their own insurance coverage. You are also responsible for avoidable hazards in your home – so make sure Ferocious Fido is safely out of the way for the day.

Plan it

Here is a big one. You need to say exactly when you want the crew to come, both the day and the time. Do you want to make the neighbours nervous or irritate the street cleaner when the cleaners' van is parked in the wrong place at the wrong time? Do you want them to arrive at 2:30 when your son's party starts at 3:00? Plan carefully beforehand. Tell them which door to use and make sure the arrangements for how they will get in and out are clear and firm even if you expect to be home – sudden emergencies, like a sick child or pet, *do* have the habit of popping up just when the builder or chimney sweep is due.

Warning: If the cleaning team doesn't have equipment and wants to use yours, I'd be a little wary.

Daily cleaners and friends might get by with this approach – but professionals, never. If they don't have the equipment, the chances are they won't know how to use it properly either.

As for quality control, use your common sense – you know approximately how long it takes you to do these household tasks, see how the pros compare. If they take too long you know something's wrong. It's best not to stand over and watch them as they work, but you'll definitely need to inspect the job afterwards and make sure it's up to scratch.

Payment

Never, never pay in advance. We pro cleaners don't expect it or deserve it. Pay when the work's complete, and you've checked it thoroughly. And, speaking of checking, always pay by cheque – it's the perfect receipt and record that the work was done, that you were satisfied, and that they actually were the ones who came and did the work. And don't agree to pay by cash because someone is 'moonlighting'. Anyone who'll cheat on tax will cheat you too.

Most cleaners can and will respond to what you expect ... demand it and you'll get it.

Becoming a professional cleaner

Of course, it's possible. If you've been working with or watching cleaning people around you at your office (and I know some of you have been muttering under your breath .,.. "Gosh, I could do that and I hear they make lots of money"), take heart. Since you've started doing housework you've found out it really is fun and easy and besides, you're fast (your wife, of course, is praising you to keep you beavering away).

Well, you're right; you can do your own thing in this business – for a few years, or for the rest of your life. If you get good at cleaning you might as well make a little profit. It's a great way to start a business the family can get involved in. I cover the basics of the process in Chapter 17 of *Is There Life After Housework?* The janitorial and cleaning industry is one of the oldest and largest professions in the world, and career opportunities abound in it.

The need and opportunities for management and leadership in this industry are endless. Few, if any, jobs available today offer greater challenge, stability and potential. Management longevity and compensations match and surpass most other industries.

Chapter Nine

FOR WOMEN'S EYES ONLY

For her eyes only

Okay fellows, take a breather, or revitalize yourself with a few straightening-up exercises and let your wife read this next section.

How any woman can feed the flame

Now that he's read this book, he won't be able to enjoy a Monday night football match or lounge around in the afternoon with a clear conscience when there's housework to be done. Once consumed with the fires of repentance we men want to, and will, do better, but for goodness sake, please leave us some pride. No matter how old we are, a little help will be appreciated – especially with things we've never done before. One steamed-up woman confronted me once and said, "If I could have one wish granted, I couldn't wait to die. I'd like to come

back and just sit in the kitchen and watch old George fumbling and groping around!"

Two weeks ago, while my wife was attending a week-long conference I performed pretty badly in the kitchen myself, and was glad she wasn't sitting there in flesh or spirit.

On the spur of the moment I decided to have an "all-fresh" dinner and made a raid on the garden and the henhouse. I'd never cooked many fresh things but I did remember she boiled the corn so I heated up a big saucepan of water. I was going to boil beetroot and some eggs, too, and thought it was a waste to dirty three saucepans at once. So I just threw the beetroot, eggs and corn all in the same boiling water. Timing never occurred to me, nor colour. I ate overcooked red corn on the cob with undercooked beetroot and Easter eggs ready three months in advance.

135

I mentioned my little meal marathon to my wife when she returned, and the next day my daughter, mother-in-law and three women from the church were all sniggering and hee-hee-ho-hoing around, and dropping little remarks my way. That was almost enough to put me off for life. If *you* get a toilet brush or squeegee into your man's fist, you ought to do everything possible to keep it there! Here are a few suggestions to keep the embers of domestic ardour burning brightly:

1. Tell us what you'd like done, instead of expecting us to read your mood and mind.

2. Be specific. Don't just wail, "I need help" without saying *what;* if we forget more than twice, you are authorised to yell. Or 'nag'.

3. Let's sit down together and decide what the priorities are. House-cleaning can be a chance to work together towards a common goal. What you learn about compromise and co-operation here will spill over into other areas of your relationship.

4. Give us a choice of several jobs to get us started. Don't give us the yuckiest job first. You could kill our desire to clean before we've even started.

5. Don't hit below the apron belt, trying to provoke us into doing, and that includes nagging. Ask graciously and we'll perform graciously.

6. No dying dog guilt trip either: eye-rolling, sighing or back-ache faking.

7. Remember we're only beginners. You may need to explain how to do it.

8. To each his own. You have your way of doing things, so let us have our way (even if you find it funny), as long as we get the job done.

9. Don't expect a miracle. Just because we've been hoarding all that housework talent for twenty or forty years, we can't redeem ourselves in a single cleaning surge.

10. Criticise privately when we ruin, break or streak something (*not* in front of the children, our friends, or your mother).

11. The power of positive feedback. Remember how miffed you were when we failed to notice the job that took you all day? Don't make us go through that; we couldn't take it. Please do notice and praise us. We are going to need it!

CHANGE

Is a magic word that can fuse joy into a hum-drum life. The act of abandoning old habits and inherited prejudices (even the ones called trad-itions) will bring an incredible sensation of free-dom. The way "they always did it" is not the way "we must always do it". Deciding and com-mitting to finding a better way is a personal glory second only to the promise of eternal life.

In this book I've tried to take a fresh new look at some calloused old bondages and some changes I've made to clean up my own act. Those changes have enriched my own life and my marriage a hundred times over, and I'm con-fident that applying the principles in these pages will do the same for you.

I went through a lot of years of life thinking flowers were sissy, that country music was the only good sound. I'd have to be caught dead at stock car racing or wearing jogging shoes. For years, I never ate olives or avocados and I couldn't stand opera; for half my life I avoided interacting with some races and organizations because of childhood conditioning. And I thought bed making, washing-up and going on little shopping errands were beneath the dignity of a real man.

Change is a marvellous force and contribution to life and it doesn't have to mean you've jettisoned your integrity. Today I order forget-me-nots fearlessly and bend my ear to Berlioz. I wear my Nikes to country fairs, listen to opera on tape (in Italian, too). And I look forward to leaving the bed neatly made and to my hands getting a little rough from doing the washing up ...

Don Aslett,
Toilet cleaner extraordinaire

Acknowledgements

I'd like to admit here that women did do some straightening up, dusting off, polishing and fetching for this book. Especially my favourite editor, Carol Cartaino, her favourite editor, Beth Franks and Tracy Monroe. As oldest daughters and big sisters they were entirely at home with the subject.

The British/Commonwealth edition was edited and designed by Helen Exley who was strongly supported by Margaret Montgomery.

Men did lend a helping hand, of course, Such as Mark Browning, who cheerfully answered all those nagging little technical questions. Then there was Butch Kriezer and Craig La Gory who came up with some top visual ideas. And David Lock, who illustrated this book. He managed to make a difficult subject appealing, even fun, against his better judgment at times.

About the author

Since his birth in a small town in southern Idaho, Don Aslett has pursued every channel of opportunity available to him. When he was fifteen, his parents put him in charge of eighty acres of the family farm; he still found time to participate enthusiastically in school athletics and church and community projects. Don left the farm for university and soon launched his own career in professional cleaning, organizing a group of students into a housecleaning and building maintenance company called Varsity Contractors. Today it is a multimillion-dollar operation that spans twelve states. Don is also the owner of a maintenance consulting company whose prime client is the huge Bell Telephone System. In addition to his ventures in the strictly business quarter, Don presents more than a hundred "Life After Housework" seminars each year and millions of people around the world have seen, heard, or read about him through TV, radio and newspaper interviews.

His first book, "Is There Life After Housework?" has sold more than half a million copies in the U.S., Britain and Australia and been translated into German, Dutch, Swedish and Hebrew. Don followed with "How to Win at Housework" and "Freedom from Clutter", both of which have passed the hundred thousand-copy mark in sales.

Have you read Don Aslett's other three books?

(Also published by Exley Publications)

Is there life after housework? (£6.95)

In his first book Don sets out to prove to the homemaker that 'long, grinding, unrewarding hours of toil are not necessary' to achieve a spotless and gleaming house. After many years experience in the contract cleaning business he is an expert in the best cost and time effective methods to use if you want your house to be a credit to you. (His methods are easy on the hands, knees and back as well!)

The equipment chapter is especially good value. Don shows which kinds of cloths, sponges, squeegees, vacuum cleaners, mops, seals and cleaners to use to tackle all household chores. He also shows you how to save money by buying equipment direct from a janitorial suppliers. In fact the book is guaranteed to save you time, money and effort and to supply you with a good deal of fun along the way.

How to win at housework (£6.95)

Don's first book was such a success that he soon had a vast fan mail from readers asking him to solve their particular cleaning problems for them. He decided to write a second book dealing with the hundred most commonly asked questions – 'do I dust or vacuum first?' – 'is there an easy way to clean venetian blinds?' – 'how do I get rid of pet pongs?' Of course he brings to this book as well as to his first, his long experience, sensible advice and his lively sense of humour.

The Secret of Freedom from Clutter (£6.95 hb, £3.95 pb)
If you answer 'yes' to any of these questions, you need this book:

1. Do you live in fear that one day someone you respect will open your cupboards – and find the awful truth?

2. Have you ever finally replaced a broken part, then carefully kept the broken bits – 'just in case'?

3. Have you ever threatened bodily harm to anyone who opens a drawer in front of guests?

4. Has most of the clobber stored away in your attic/cellar/garage/garden shed lain there for years – unused?

Save your sanity – not your cardboard boxes, souvenirs and old shoes. In *Freedom from Clutter*, Don Aslett shows how insidious clutter really is. It not only crowds out cellars and attics, it blunts our effectiveness as people. If you are forever looking after, sorting, dusting, storing and insuring the clobber in your life, how can you ever be free? Clutter, quite simply, is bad for you. It doesn't enrich life, it robs you of free time. A giant collection of things simply exhausts your physical and emotional energy.

Through anecdotes, charts and quizzes, Don delves into all the junk areas, in the home and in the office, offering practical ways of dealing with the menace of clutter. With a hilarious 'Junkee's identity test' he helps you assess just how bad your problem is; he lists the hundred and one feeble excuses for hanging on to clutter and gives you hundreds of practical ideas for getting rid of clutter.

For all who have waged war on clutter and lost, here is the inspiration to get the job done once and for all!

All three books may be bought at good bookshops or ordered direct from: Exley Publications Ltd, 16 Chalk Hill, Watford, Herts WD1 4BN. Please add 95p to your order to cover postage and packing.